TOWARD
LIBERATION

TOWARD LIBERATION

EDUCATIONAL PRACTICES ROOTED IN ACTIVISM, HEALING, AND LOVE

JAMILAH PITTS

BEACON PRESS ▪ BOSTON

BEACON PRESS
Boston, Massachusetts
www.beacon.org

Beacon Press books
are published under the auspices of
the Unitarian Universalist Association of Congregations.

26 25 24 23   8 7 6 5 4 3 2 1

This book is printed on acid-free paper that meets the uncoated paper
ANSI/NISO specifications for permanence as revised in 1992.

Text design and composition by Kim Arney

Excerpts from Anaiyah's Poetry Anthology
by Anaiyah Smith are printed here with permission.

Library of Congress Cataloging-in-Publication-Data is available for this title.
ISBN: 978-0-8070-1484-4; e-book: 978-0-8070-1485-1

For My Mother
My First Teacher

Your sacrifices and unwavering, steadfast
commitment to ensuring that your children
are educated and thereby free will
never go unnoticed

CONTENTS

FOREWORD

In *Toward Liberation*, educator, activist, and cultural worker Jamilah Pitts provides an elegant guide to returning education to its rightful place as a tool for liberation. While much of formal education has branded itself a tool of social justice, sometimes equity, and, more recently, anti-Black racism, this book provides a fresh, accessible, and grounding text in what is required to engage education as a tool for liberation. This book is a guidebook for remaking teacher education programs and professional learning communities to marshal education as a tool for liberation.

Leveraging her own journey as an educator, Jamilah provides specific examples of pedagogy that centers the knowledge traditions of people of color. While this may seem like an obvious inclusion, it is, in fact, far from normal, let alone normalized. Jamilah grounds the reader in the fact that the United States empire is deeply invested in many intertwined lies, and education is one of the strongest tools to unlearn these lies so that collectivity, curiosity, and ancestral wisdom can take shape in the place of lies.

One of the many strong threads in Jamilah's book is the role of truthtelling. Grounded in James Baldwin's work, specifically his speech "A Talk to Teachers," Jamilah centers truthtelling as a praxis for liberation. Jamilah speaks unapologetically about what this meant to her as an educator of Black children, yet her message is clear: liberation must be for all or it is simply not liberation. Interestingly, Baldwin and Audre Lorde, another scholar whom Jamilah turns to and lifts up, had a legendary conversation, published in *Essence* magazine, in 1984. In that conversation, Lorde attempts several times to show Baldwin that growing up in a society in which racism, ableism, misogynoir, and racial capitalism are the forces that even men and women of color, Black men and women, can weaponize oppressions to be wielded against each other. This legendary conversation is found throughout the pages of this powerful book.

Jamilah doesn't need to cite this conversation, although her citations open many doors for readers, and yet her writing is drenched in the beauty that resides in working every day for education for liberation. In a stunningly short space, Jamilah pushes readers to understand how to not cede power to reductive policies, how to open curriculum to students, and how to keep central an awareness of the intersectional oppressions that so many Black and Brown populations experience.

When I began my days as a teacher, I was familiar with several books about, in essence, how to "survive" the first one hundred days or the first year. They tended to focus on classroom discipline or management, consistency above all else, and structure. Reading this book obliterates that low ceiling for teachers, both beginning and experienced, inviting them into the more meaningful work of leveraging opportunities for growth. I will not falsely equate teaching for liberation with teaching for control. They speak a different language altogether. Jamilah's book takes its place alongside contemporary classics such as Carla Shalaby's *Troublemakers: Lessons in Freedom from Young Children at School* and Theresa Perry and Lisa Delpit's edited volume, *The Real Ebonics Debate: Power, Language, and the Education of African-American Children.* Jamilah's book is in this fine company because she positions the act of teaching as always political, always with liberatory potential, and always with the potential for social change.

For those of you who enrolled in teacher education because you loved school, this book will help you to see what was going terribly wrong while you were getting all A's and taking every AP course offered. If you preferred libraries to classrooms, this book speak sings your song. If you, like so many of our educators, have been stretched beyond exhaustion, this book will return you to your core purpose of staying human so that you can teach.

I had the pleasure of teaching a course in which Jamilah and her peers did a close reading of Baldwin's "A Talk to Teachers." She was then, and is now, not satisfied with platitudes about reaching just one child or reveling in a light bulb of comprehension. Jamilah has always had a keen sense that no standards or curriculum could possibly speak to the needs that teachers have so they can best serve not only their students but also society. The project is no smaller than education for liberation, every day.

This book is a beacon for caregivers, students, and educators who sense that learning must be bigger than adequate yearly progress or satisfactory attendance records. Schooling has always been a contested place in the United States, stratified and exclusionary by design. Jamilah's guidance brings us to the place of home that learning rightfully claims. We are raised through learning. While there is no magic guidebook for the first one hundred days, this book is a guide for the integrated wellness of teachers. I cannot think of a time when we needed it more.

—Leigh Patel

TOWARD
LIBERATION

ON BALDWIN'S "A TALK TO TEACHERS"

James Baldwin's "A Talk to Teachers," delivered in 1963 in New York City to a group of teachers, came on the heels of some of the most devastating and destructive crimes against Black bodies in the 1950s and '60s. Baldwin addressed teachers in the aftermath of the brutal and cold murder of Emmett Till, the bombing of the 16th Street Baptist Church, which killed four young Black girls, and other horrendous acts of violence and terror enacted against the Black community during this time. Baldwin admonished teachers, eloquently stating, "So any citizen of this country who figures himself* as responsible—and particularly those of you who deal with the minds and hearts of young people—must be prepared to 'go for broke.'"[1]

Baldwin must have been aware of the ways that schools mirror society and how teachers and educators either perpetuate systems of oppression and racial terror or use their position to resist, to interrupt, and to disrupt. But one might also suspect, given Baldwin's hopeful stance (despite his rightful consistent critiques of America) and given its proximity to children, the teaching profession represented the greatest form of hope.

Anyone dealing with the minds of young people, Baldwin suggests, must be willing to "go for broke." For Baldwin, educators, particularly teachers, stood—and still stand—on dangerous and vulnerable front lines. The job of a teacher, each day,

---

*Acknowledging here the lack of inclusivity of this language, particularly given the time and lens through which I am writing. I submit to readers to consider this language instead: (herself, himself, their self)

is to influence, shape, and mold the minds and hearts of students. Students who will become the human beings who affect society, craft policy, and work against (or perpetuate) harmful dominant narratives. Those who will stand against human rights crises and violations and cure diseases. Teachers are not solely in the business of curating learning spaces. Teachers are entrenched in an art form of interrupting, disrupting, encouraging, healing, and liberating.

WHY BALDWIN?

In crafting this text, I did not hesitate to begin with James Baldwin's "A Talk to Teachers." I have yet to encounter another writer or seminal text that has shaped my practice and life as an educator more than Baldwin's. Although the work of James Baldwin may seem like an unlikely choice to ground a book about education, it is not. His works often focused on the Black experience in America. He wrote from a raw and critical place and examined the state of race relations through a lens that made it difficult, nearly impossible, to refute the experiences of Black people in America during the time that he wrote. His truth reverberates today.

The social and political climate in which Baldwin delivered his address is not vastly different from the current society that we are teaching, living, and operating in. Although students in the 1960s entered schools with the weight of the world on their shoulders, many of our students, particularly Black children, enter learning spaces today with stories and lived experiences that mirror those of the 1960s. They are able to draw comparisons between the murders of Emmett Till and Trayvon Martin and Mike Brown. Young people can draw connections between lynching and mass incarceration and question the progress of our country's justice system. Children in some communities associate immigration authorities with stark fear. Our children can understand the hateful rhetoric of a former president who cares very little about their communities. Students can point to the similarities between the historical oppression of women and the Me Too movement, and cry today. And although students know and recognize advancements regarding marriage equality, they must also reckon with the increase in transphobia and homophobia within their communities and the recurrence of violence and oppression against women. Many students deal regularly with the brutal realities of economic disparity, violence, drug abuse, mental illness, rape, sexual abuse, abandonment, and other forms of trauma. They do not magically rid themselves of this awareness, nor of their trauma, when they walk through our school doors or join our learning spaces.

And, so as Baldwin urges, we must be willing to "go for broke." We must be willing to engage in our work and practices in a way that meets the needs of our students, as they are.

MY "WHY," CALL AND INVITATION

What we have been taught, what has pained us, and what we believe about ourselves drive, in many ways, who we are and who we choose to become. My decision to become a teacher was birthed from a place of remembering where I felt I most belonged as a child. The choice to say yes to the call of teaching stemmed from a place of deep pain. Each year, as a classroom teacher, I saw in the faces of my students that which pained me most—the murders and incarceration of classmates, an oppressive "justice" system, the all-consuming impacts of growing up in a poor, Black community. My fearlessness as an advocate, as an educator, and as a leader stemmed from remembering the treatment of my brother, the pain he felt as a Black boy, and the insecurities my sister and I long carried as Black girls growing up in a poor environment. My unwavering belief in the power of young people and the need for educators to place anti-racism and liberation at the core of all that we do came from an understanding of the ways that our communities, our schools, our neighborhoods, the words we heard, and the images we saw in the media were intentionally designed to destroy us.

I think often of my classmates who have been murdered and of others who are serving life sentences in prison. I think of my family members who struggle with illness, such as drug addiction, and I consider a world, structures, laws, policies, and institutions that have been created—by people—to leave other people in despair.

I also became a teacher because I *love* Blackness, I *love* children, especially children who look like me, and I possessed an early love for learning. Although my mother never attended college or had a formal education, she was rooted in the ethics and principles of Black womanhood, Black excellence, and Black joy. She is unapologetic in her role as my first teacher. I remember the days she would take off work so she could be one of the first mothers in line for the school lottery. We—my siblings and I—had no other choice than to attend public schools in Columbus, Ohio, but my mother made sure that they were the *best* public schools in the district. I entered kindergarten more than academically prepared because my mother instilled a love of reading in our home. And Black history—my understanding and knowledge of where and whence I came—was evident in the music we listened to, the Black leaders on our stamps, the art in our home, and the movies and TV shows we watched. I did not have a white teacher until I was in fifth grade, and she was a wonderful teacher. Still, before fifth grade, I was loved, nurtured, and encouraged by Black teachers, Black women who required that we know the words of the Black national anthem, who made us recite, each day, "I am somebody," teachers who encouraged us to dream and who truly *loved* us.

My call to teach became cemented as a high school student and later as a student at Spelman College when it became clear that education was either a tool of oppression or a tool of freedom. By high school, I had lost classmates to gun violence and prison. The same children who had sat alongside me and recited "I am somebody."

Our divergent paths were never lost on me, and the pain—the ability to see this world for what it is—set me ablaze to do something about it.

I believe in the power of teachers and in the power of education. I believe we must disrupt, that we must interrupt, that we must possess the deepest integrity, that we must operate not from places of ego but that we must tell the truth at all costs, that we must be in service to our children, and that we are charged, entrusted, with other people's children and play a role as guides to what our world will become. In a world that is laced with, and sickly praises, forms of domination—phobias, racism, sexism, and capitalism—we have to be ruthless in our efforts to transform and liberate. Teaching for me is a form of activism, and I urge educators to join me in this practice.

My educational and teaching pedagogy over the past decade has been founded on the tenets of educational practices rooted in activism, liberation, healing, and love. I seek to honor and expand the activists, authors, scholars and educators that have come before me in this lineage of work, such as Paulo Freire, bell hooks, Anna Julia Cooper, Ella Baker, Gloria Ladson-Billings, and Audre Lorde. And in this text, this offering, I guide educators through this process in hopes that we will step more deeply into our profession, our art form, in ways that *truly* make the world a better place. This text walks teachers through the tenets I have practiced and believe are necessary to move us *toward liberation*. Teachers must understand that liberatory teaching is rooted in the tenets shown in the Liberatory Teaching Wheel (figure 1.1):

- centers healing
- centers activism and social justice
- is truthtelling

FIGURE 1.1 Liberatory Teaching Wheel

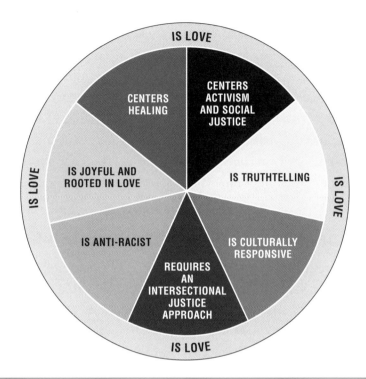

- is culturally responsive
- requires an intersectional justice approach
- is anti-racist
- is joyful and rooted in love

When I began crafting this text, I did so out of a belief in the power of education, particularly to promote healing, empathy, and social justice. I wanted to encourage educators to use this platform as a mechanism and vehicle for transformation, social change, and love. And then we entered the year 2020, which presented us with two major pandemics: the global health pandemic that we were all forced to navigate and grow through, and as the year wore on, the (long overdue) awakening to the pandemic that has existed since the inception of this country. This pandemic is the intentional and deliberate violence against Black bodies across the African diaspora and particularly within the United States.

Now, this work, this offering of my heart, which is rooted in my experiences and in success stories from my time with my students, is highly controversial. Today, the teaching profession is a battlefield, full of contradictory practices and beliefs. On the one hand, there are measures to implement and sustain anti-racism, antibias, and anti-oppressive practices, and on the other, there exists deeply performative measures rooted in capitalism and ego and movements to work against truthtelling and the liberation most needed in schools. I extend this offering, *still*.

As a Black woman, I am concerned chiefly with the ways that people are harmed within and under systems of oppression deliberately designed to uphold white supremacist ideas and to relegate to the margins of society people who do not fit into ideas of whiteness. I am concerned with the ways that ideas around whiteness and superiority are baked into our schools and are harmful to our children.

MY APPROACH: HEALING, WOMANISM, INTERSECTIONALITY → LIBERATION

Although anti-racism is integral and largely a part of the foundation of the work that I do within the field of education, liberation is, ultimately, where I want to see us moved to. I share often, in my practice with schools, that the true goal ought to be liberation and that to do so we must use an intersectional justice lens. This means that we must consider all of the ways that people of the Global Majority, especially Black women, are harmed due to multiple and intersecting forms of oppression. As a Black woman in America, my lived experience positions me to understand this dire need. Efforts to mitigate racism without addressing patriarchy or sexism deny and overlook the uniquely harmful experience of being Black women and girls. Therefore, my work is situated heavily within a womanist practice and lens.

The term *womanist* was coined by writer Alice Walker to account for the ways that the early waves of feminism excluded the experiences of Black women and were, therefore, not focused on ensuring that all women were able to be free and thrive.[2] A womanist approach in liberatory education is both necessary and critical. I long for our world to arrive at a place where we are as concerned about the experiences of Black women as we are other marginalized groups. The power of a womanist approach is that it is expansive; it is rooted in abolitionist pedagogy; it results in the liberation of all who are harmed by oppression because it positions us to consider those most oppressed within any society. I love and champion the work of Audre Lorde, for example, because her experience, writing, and activism requires that we consider the intersectional experiences of Black women. Although anti-racism is one step, a liberation mindset encompasses intersectional justice and accounts for the varying and simultaneous ways that people, especially Black women and girls, are oppressed within a system. A womanist lens moves us toward collective liberation because in considering the multiple aspects of a Black woman's identity that may cause her/them to experience harm (this might include racism in addition to sexism, classism, transphobia, homophobia, and disability injustice), we are able to move toward a place of collective liberation and healing. A liberation pedagogy driven by womanism requires educators to consider the whole child and intersectional forms of oppression and harm, and sets us up to work toward liberation.

Within this text, I call upon educators to reorient our stance and our role within the practice and work of liberation. I urge us to consider the ways that we yield power and privilege because we teach and influence the minds of the most precious beings in our societies and communities—young people.

The goal is liberation.

Pedagogy rooted in liberation recognizes the ways that school systems uphold inequalities and oppressive practices. Therefore, educators whose pedagogy is rooted in liberation seek to tell the truth, to heal, to liberate. This requires courage, the ability to tell and hear the truth, the ability to continuously act, learn, and grow a deep, deep return to the source of self, all life, and all beings—love.

A NOTE ON MY FALLIBILITY AND MY GROWTH

I hope one day humanity will have evolved to be in a place where a text of this nature is no longer needed, and if it is needed, I trust that educators, scholars, writers, thinkers, and doers will have added to the practice of liberation in schools in ways that surpass my offerings herein. I trust, truly, that the young people we teach and lead today know better and will push each of us to do better.

This book is a combination of my lived experiences as a student growing up in a (monetarily) poor Black environment, my reflections on my childhood and experiences as a Black girl in school, and my practice as an educator—largely as a teacher, then a school leader, and now as an entrepreneur and consultant who trains teachers and leaders—over the past decade.

I know that there are pieces I have missed or overlooked and aspects of my practice and thought that are still evolving. In that spirit, as I offer guidance for teachers on what it means to heal, to operate from a place of love in the pursuit of transformation, activism, and liberation, I recognize that I am imperfect and that I, too, will miss the mark in some ways.

Some of the reflections, guidance, and practices are based on wins in the classroom and in my work as an educator, but many others are based on losses—the days I did not get it right, the times I was not the best teacher or colleague, the times I created harm and had to step back, reflect, and seek ways to do and be better. I cannot write about or speak of love, healing, and practices of domination without acknowledging the ways that I must continue to heal and the areas in my life where I can cultivate more love.

This book feels nearly impossible to finish, because in a pursuit of liberation, which I believe is love actualized, we are never finished.

CHAPTER 1

TEACHING AS TRUTHTELLING

If we can honor teaching as an art form, then we can honor and uphold the commitments of the responsibility of the artist to tell the truth, to disrupt the status quo, to dismantle the systems that bind Black bodies, to "vomit the anguish up." In an article describing the work of artists, Baldwin observes, "All art is a kind of confession, more or less oblique. All artists, if they are to survive, are forced, at last, to tell the whole story, to vomit the anguish up."[1] Teachers must be willing to take this stance if we are to teach children in ways that will ultimately lead to a better, healed, free society and world.

Is this not the ultimate goal of education?

As a child, I had several Black teachers. The beauty of growing up in a community filled with Black people, Black mothers, and other Black children is that I was not taught—solely—to pander to nor to desire whiteness. My mother and my first schoolteachers taught me the truth about Black beauty, Black excellence, and the power of my own dreaming as a Black girl. Thanks to Ms. Jackson, my kindergarten teacher, I learned the words to the Black national anthem, "Lift Every Voice and Sing," just as I learned the Pledge of Allegiance and the words to "The Star-Spangled Banner." From books, I learned about exceptional, intelligent, courageous Black people such as Ruby Bridges, the young Black girl who helped integrate segregated schools in the American South; the athlete Wilma Rudolph; and the inventor Garrett Morgan. By second grade, I had an additional understanding that Black people had *absolutely* resisted when they were enslaved. Before I encountered the docile, passive depiction of enslaved people that history books so often depict, I had already learned the truth about my ancestors.

This nation has been created and sustained by lies. And the debate over measures to promote and sustain anti-racism within the past couple of years reveals the strained relationship with truthtelling that this country has long had. Lies that regard white people as superior, while relegating people of the Global Majority—historically resilient people, including Black people, Black women, communities of color, and Indigenous people—to the pits of history, silencing our creations, innovations, intellects, and contributions of excellence. There are the lies that suggest that Black people have contributed nothing to this world, that we are violent and lazy, when, in fact, we are excellent and have built everything. And these lies are perpetuated, intentionally, in what we teach and what we choose to silence in our curriculum, in what we maintain through our ignorance, and in the discourse we refuse to have with our students. Teachers perpetuate lies when we do not teach about what this world, what this country, has done to the oppressed and when we do not teach stories and current examples of excellence, resistance, and joy. We perpetuate lies when we refuse to depart from white dominant patriarchal ideologies and philosophies that surround what it means to "teach well" in this country.

Teaching truth. What does that even mean? One critical component that educators have to wrestle with is the idea that systems of oppression are often sustained, perpetuated, and passed down through teaching. This may seem extreme, even radical (we should aim to get at the *root* of things; that is what the word "radical" actually means), but it is true. Teaching truth begins with the acknowledgment of our role as teachers in movements of resistance, in the practice of liberation. The ways we uphold or dismantle truths play a role in either dismantling oppression or perpetuating it. We must also consider that our practice is an art form, and as a result it comes with great responsibility and should be subversive. We ought to be required to teach our content fully, dissect our own beliefs, and include the voices of the marginalized and the silenced within the narratives and forms of history about this nation that are often regurgitated. We must speak truth to power in our classrooms. We must be vigilant about not perpetuating oppression by continuing to teach the lies that sustain stories of white dominance, patriarchy, phobias, and other isms that have been designed to raise and honor a truth that is rooted in the erasure, dehumanization, and destruction of people deemed inferior within any society.

Teachers are artists and practitioners. And it is important that when shifting practices and applications, we begin with a few realizations. The first being that anti-racist, anti-oppression, liberatory teaching cannot be trimmed down to a checklist or rubric of practices. The deepest work, the deepest shifts, require internal work. This is where teachers must begin: with themselves, examining their own practices and beliefs, interrogating their truths, and allowing this process to shift and mold their practices.

Truth is a broad and somewhat deeply abstract subject. The idea of "teaching truth" or truthtelling through teaching begs many questions: What is truth? Whose truth? And what does this have to do with teaching? This concept of teaching truth, for me, in a narrower sense, pertains to the ways in which we honor our students, their histories, their identities, and what they have come to believe about the world. Teaching the truth means uplifting the experiences and stories of the marginalized and silenced and acknowledging the lies that have been taught in this country, specifically those that sustain and perpetuate white dominance, patriarchy, and other methods of erasure, domination, and oppression. This form of teaching, rooted in lies, includes, but certainly is not limited to: a history that praises or overlooks entirely colonization and the killing and erasure of Indigenous people and culture, the silencing and demonizing of women of color, the experiences of the poor, the journeys of queer people in this country, the degradation and dehumanization of Black bodies, and the lack of giving credit to whom credit is due. Teaching truth requires centering the truth about the resilience and excellence of communities and cultures that are often demonized or silenced, cultures of the Global Majority. The act of teaching as reclaiming, as exposing lies, as honoring the backgrounds, experiences, and knowledge that students bring into our classrooms, as centering the voices of groups that are silenced—as opposed to continuing a pattern of centering the voices, experiences, and false beliefs about whiteness and white people—is teaching as truthtelling. It is raising critical consciousness, developing the sorts of critical minds that Baldwin admonishes no society wants to have around.[2]

It means offering narratives about people of the Global Majority and resistance rooted in facts rather than myths about docility and passivity. It means reexamining where Black history begins in our textbooks in order to teach the whole lives of Black sheroes. History loves to diminish the roles and lives of Black sheroes and heroes. Dr. Martin Luther King, for example, is lauded for being a nonviolent leader, which is a part of the truth, but his leadership also included radicalism, critiquing and working against poverty, and other ideas and philosophies that rendered him violent, unlovable, and threatening. We cannot ignore that, even still, the man was murdered because he posed such a deep threat to a society and world that wants to see systems of oppression, erasure, and silencing prevail. The recounting of history surrounding Dr. King must also center the work of Ella Baker and other Black women whose voices, motives, and strategies both built and sustained the civil rights movement. It is having the conversation around the place of intersectionality and how movements of Black resistance often ignore the contributions of Black women. In the essay "Love as the Practice of Freedom," bell hooks speaks to this inability to examine the full truths in recounting, specifically, the role of sexism among Black male leaders in movements of Black liberation:

> It has always puzzled me that women and men who spend a lifetime working to resist and oppose one form of domination can be systematically supporting another. I have been puzzled by powerful visionary black male leaders who can speak and act passionately in resistance to racial domination and accept and embrace sexist domination of women. . . .
>
> The sixties Black Power movement shifted away from that love ethic. The emphasis was now more on power. And it is not surprising that the sexism that had always undermined the black liberation struggle intensified, that a misogynist approach to women became central as the equation of freedom with patriarchal manhood became a norm among black political leaders, almost all of whom were male.[3]

Truthtelling in teaching means centering the contributions of Black women and Black queer women to units on resistance and critically examining the role of patriarchy and capitalism. Truthtelling must require a holistic and intersectional lens if we are to move *toward collective liberation*.

Truthtelling as a vehicle to achieve liberation, however, will not just happen on its own. Teachers, education leaders, teacher preparation programs, and institutions must be deliberate. The strategies for teaching truth must be as intentional, nuanced, and sharp as those that allow educational systems and schools to maintain beliefs, practices, and policies that are rooted in lies about white superiority. In an effort for teachers to commit fully to liberation, we must operate with the understanding that Audre Lorde has provided us with. "The master's tools," she writes, "will never dismantle the master's house. They may allow us temporarily to beat him at his own game, but they will never enable us to bring about genuine change."[4] Many, including BIPOC (Black, Indigenous, people of color) people, believe that systems of oppression can be overturned and overthrown if we merely use the tools of oppressors, if we study how oppression is perpetuated and then use the same measures and means for our own gain and success. I once worked for Black leaders who believed this, and this belief held by Black leaders is especially dangerous. It is misguided. Bettina Love deepens Lorde's argument, specifically regarding schools, in *We Want to Do More Than Survive: Abolitionist Teaching and the Pursuit of Educational Freedom*. To permanently beat the oppressor at their game, we cannot rely on the master's tools. We must dream radically. We must work toward abolition. We must do something different. Love captures the necessity of freedom dreaming in schools: "We must struggle together not only to reimagine schools but to build new schools that we are taught to believe are impossible: schools based on intersectional justice, anti-racism, love, healing, and joy. . . . Abolitionist teaching starts with freedom dreaming, dreams grounded in a critique of injustice."[5]

Teachers must be deeply thoughtful and imaginative as we seek to think about, think through, and plan for methods of schooling and teaching that are not aimed at recreating systems of oppression but are rooted in what it truly means to liberate. Certainly, we cannot do this if we do not have space to dream and to create anew. We cannot do this if we are unwell, overburdened, tired, and physically drained— but I will get to this in the chapters on healing and self-care.

Teachers seeking to center truthtelling must go through a process of examining *their* truths and study other methods of truthtelling, including those of their students. Teachers must work to center the voices and experiences of groups that have historically been silenced or whose narratives have been taught in ways that are one-sided in order to promote a white dominant agenda.

I had a friend once explain to me that teaching is a deeply humanistic profession. That who we are, what we believe, and that which pains and excites us shape who we are as teachers, what we teach, how we teach, and what we come to believe as teachers. Another brilliant teacher and educator explained that what made one of our colleagues so powerful, so dear, was their ability to pour into our children that which this world had robbed from them. Teaching truth must begin with teachers diving deeply into who they are, the beliefs they hold, and then constantly examining and reexamining those beliefs. This must be continuous work whereby educators commit to a practice of understanding that what they know to be true will, in many respects, continue to evolve.

TAKE TIME FOR SELF-REFLECTION

One of the first steps we must take in teaching truth is examining what we believe about the world and where children of power, children of the Global Majority, and their histories are situated within those beliefs. For example, if a teacher, especially someone who is teaching students of the Global Majority, feels that it is OK to teach that Christopher Columbus "discovered" America, that teacher's molding and thinking has to be confronted, disrupted, and guided in the direction of truth. For reference, I draw on some of the links between my own truths and how these connect to my practice. In figure 1.2, I have created and organized a model, beginning with an example of my self-reflection. Teachers can then use this model to think about their own truths and how this translates to their practice.

FIGURE 1.2 Self-Reflection for Teachers

SELF-REFLECTION QUESTIONS	HOW MY BELIEFS SHAPE HOW I ACT	HOW MY BELIEFS SHAPE HOW I REFUSE TO ACT

• Who am I? As an educator? As a person?
• What do I believe the role of an educator to be? What responsibilities do I have?
• What is my educational philosophy? Why do I believe that? Where do those ideas come from?
	My upbringing in an all-Black family and in all-Black communities deeply shape who I am and what I believe as a teacher. I also grew up in poverty, where I experienced and witnessed firsthand the links between racism, crime, poverty, and addiction. I am, therefore, an educator and a leader who is deeply committed to anti-racism, social justice, human rights, healing, and actions that eradicate all forms of oppression.
	    I believe that education can be used as an instrument of oppression or as a vehicle for liberation, freedom, and healing. I believe that what we teach one another and what we teach children links directly to the policies we create, the morals and principles we hold, how we act, how we interact with one another, what breaks our hearts, and what compels us to action.
	    These ideas come from my lived experiences as a Black woman in this country, the experiences of my loved ones, the teachings of my ancestors, and my experiences as a student in all-Black learning environments in my formative years. The pain and trauma I have experienced, most of which are directly linked to racism, poverty, and sexism, have deeply shaped these ideas.
		I believe that silence and inaction are dangerous tools. I believe and know that educators' silence perpetuates oppression and harm and that our words as teachers have power.
		    I am committed to disrupting and dismantling all forms of oppression, especially those tied directly to my lived experience.
		    I refuse to be silent about systems of oppression and the ways that schools, specifically, uphold them. And I believe in using curriculum as a weapon and tool to deepen students' critical consciousness so that they are equipped to identify and name oppression and determine how they wish to work against it.

FIGURE 1.2 Self-Reflection for Teachers, *continued*

SELF-REFLECTION QUESTIONS	HOW MY BELIEFS SHAPE HOW I ACT	HOW MY BELIEFS SHAPE HOW I REFUSE TO ACT
▪ What is my truth as it relates to teaching? ▪ What do I believe about what I am teaching? ▪ What are the lies that I uphold and perhaps pass on to my students, based on what I teach?	I believe that teaching is a vehicle that is used to either disrupt oppression or to uphold it. I truly do not believe that there is an in-between, and I believe that there exists content and materials in our communities, in our histories, and in our families that lead to liberation in ways that "traditional" models of teaching do not. Therefore, as a teacher and leader, I always seek to center what I believe about the world in what and how I teach. I strive to create space for students to push back, ask questions, and tell their truth. I approach all content through a critical lens, and I ask students to think about who is silenced and why they are silenced. There were times as a teacher when I bought into what the world said about Black women. I corrected students who I thought were being "disrespectful" for speaking their truths because I had not yet unpacked the ways in which I had internalized my own oppression and passed that on to my students.	The more that I learn, the more that I act, evolve, apologize, and do better. Each time. I refuse to know better and not to do better.
▪ What are the truths that I have been taught? ▪ What are the truths that I have learned about my history, my culture, my language, my people?	Because I have been taught and continue to learn about the beauty of my people and of other BIPOC, I continue to operate fully within my power. I continue to write, teach, and speak in ways that honor the excellence of Black people. I continue to find ways to tap into that power and to evolve. And when I am teaching teachers or teaching students, I share those aspects of my journey with them, and I encourage them to do the same.	I refuse to teach in ways that center white dominance or white ways of being as superior and particularly at the expense of the contribution and histories of people of the Global Majority. As an English teacher, I refused to teach a syllabus full of only all-white texts; I refused to allow students—including white students—to believe that Black people did not contribute incredible things to this world and to this country.

continues

FIGURE 1.2 Self-Reflection for Teachers (*continued*)

SELF-REFLECTION QUESTIONS	HOW MY BELIEFS SHAPE HOW I ACT	HOW MY BELIEFS SHAPE HOW I REFUSE TO ACT
▪ What are my truths as they relate to people? ▪ What do I believe about people who belong to protected classes (poor people, Black people, Indigenous people, trans people, queer people, and people with disabilities)?	I believe that people who are different from us offer us ways to understand the world and ourselves more deeply. I believe in the beauty of *all* human beings. I also believe that it is important to acknowledge that people who are marginalized are oppressed intentionally and deliberately. I believe that examining and understanding oppression, taking a close look at the ugliest parts of our humanity, helps us to forge forward paths rooted in liberation. We cannot heal what we refuse to acknowledge or discuss.	I refuse to be close-minded to ideas, beliefs, and experiences that are different from my own. I refuse to be silent about oppression. I refuse to ignore those who are relegated to the margins and to participate in systems, beliefs, structures, and ways of being that further perpetuate oppressive cycles.

EXAMINE YOUR THINKING USING CRITICAL THEORIES

One of my most powerful experiences of dissecting and reflecting on the knowledge that I had been fed came during one of my required first-year courses at Spelman College. The purpose of the course, entitled African Diaspora and the World, was to reteach and reclaim Black history, particularly through a womanist or Black feminist lens. Its sole purpose was to expose the lies that had been taught about Black history, particularly lies that existed due to the omission of facts from K–12 educational history textbooks. In this course, I learned about the diaspora and gained a deeper understanding of the transatlantic slave trade. I also learned about the beauty and power of African and Indigenous peoples prior to their enslavement and colonization and how their beauty and power endured. And this was the foundation for all of my courses at Spelman College. What was most important was that not only did my collegiate experience expose the lies and replace those lies with truth, but it also gave me the tools and the language to be able to research, study, disrupt, write, teach, and counteract narratives that would seek to destroy this level of understanding and freedom.

The practice of relearning and reclaiming history is massive, as the fiber and DNA of this country requires stories and a false premise that encourages children and adults alike to believe that Black people, Black women, queer people, Indigenous people, and the poor are inferior, and these beliefs, these lies around our inferiority, are sustained through what is taught in schools and other places of learning. They are sustained in some teachings of the Church, in limited or one-sided ideas about how life came to be in the sciences, even in the myths about the inferiority of Black people having roots in the sciences. One of the largest lies, we all know, are those about how this country was "discovered," which is further perpetuated by the literal, and now historical, erasure of Indigenous people, their narratives, and their stories. And worse, there are now movements and legislation in some places that deem truthtelling as divisive or un-American. It's another tactic to preserve harmful ideas, practices, and lies rooted in false notions that white people are superior.

Developing a critical consciousness can seem like a daunting task. Essentially, this process is complex and uncomfortable because we are tasked with thinking more deeply and asking questions about the world, about what we know, and about what we know about what we know. This is what Baldwin describes as the crucial paradox of education. Furthermore, we are living during a time now when those seeking to perpetuate various forms of harm are creating movements to interrupt and vilify these types of thinking that lead to liberation for those most harmed by systems of oppression and degradation. Critical literacies and theories provide a framework through which teachers can begin to think differently about erasure and truthtelling. *And* critical theories provide each of us with a framework to develop our own critical consciousness. The purpose of critical theories—Black feminist thought, critical race, Marxist, queer, and LatCrit—allows teachers, and students, to think differently about *everything* that we are learning. The theories require that teachers be thoughtful about who is telling the story, if they are rooted in a dominant lie, the perspectives or viewpoints that may be silenced in the story or content. This is one of the most practical ways that teachers can begin to open their minds, and subsequently, those of their students, to thinking and acting in ways that lead toward liberation. Figure 1.3 lists a few examples of critical theories and some questions for educators to consider.

FIGURE 1.3 An Educator's Guide to Critical Theories

THEORY	WHAT THESE THEORISTS ASK US TO CONSIDER	SELF-EXAMINATION: HOW CAN TEACHERS USE THE THEORIES AS A TOOL FOR THEIR SELF-EXAMINATION?	QUESTIONS TO INFLUENCE EDUCATIONAL PRACTICES
Critical Race Theory	• How do systems, structures, institutions, and policies promote and uphold racism? • How are people of the Global Majority being impacted, disenfranchised, and oppressed? • How does this uphold myths about white superiority, particularly at the expense of people of the Global Majority? • How are Black people being harmed? Relegated to the margins? Being discriminated against? • What do I understand about critical race theory? What research and reading have I done to understand what it is and what it is not?	• Teachers can begin to ask and answer these questions for themselves. First, these questions can be applied to their own doings, thoughts, philosophies, and beliefs. Teachers can also pose these questions for students to consider and come back to as they are reading or absorbing from various texts, entering into discussions, and writing. Teachers can model what it looks like to answer these questions.	• What does this text, content, message, etc. suggest about people of the Global Majority? • What systems within schools perpetuate racism? • How can I center anti-racism?
Feminist Theory	• How do systems, structures, institutions, policies, and the media promote and reinforce sexist, patriarchal ideas? • How are women being disenfranchised and oppressed? • How does this uphold myths about male superiority?	• All teachers, even teachers who identify as women, can begin to think about and observe the world through this lens. • All teachers can begin with defining these terms, then move into sharing the questions as a foundational way of thinking about the world and the content they are provided to study, examine, apply, etc.	• What does this text, content, message, etc. suggest about women? • What systems within schools perpetuate sexism? • Where does feminism miss the mark, particularly as it pertains to women of color? • How can I be certain to embed an intersectional lens?

FIGURE 1.3 An Educator's Guide to Critical Theories, *continued*

THEORY	WHAT THESE THEORISTS ASK US TO CONSIDER	SELF-EXAMINATION: HOW CAN TEACHERS USE THE THEORIES AS A TOOL FOR THEIR SELF-EXAMINATION?	QUESTIONS TO INFLUENCE EDUCATIONAL PRACTICES
Marxist Theory	▪ How does socioeconomic status affect people's lives, particularly the lives of poor people? ▪ How are systems set up to benefit the rich and promote capitalism at the expense of the poor? ▪ What rights do poor people have? ▪ How do poverty, racism, and sexism intersect to create especially painful conditions and lived experiences for women and girls of color? ▪ What is capitalism? ▪ In what ways might capitalism harm communities and people, especially people who are poor? ▪ Who was Karl Marx and what did he actually believe? Why was there such a deep resistance to his work and beliefs? ▪ How might this theory and thinking support a deeper commitment to actions rooted in compassion, empathy, and humanity?	▪ How does your socioeconomic status impact who you are, what you believe, and how you teach? Does this impact where you teach and who you interact with and gain knowledge from? How does your socioeconomic status dictate what you determine as truth and how you view truths that may be different from your own? ▪ What beliefs and thoughts do you hold about people who are poor and why they are poor?	Teachers can actually pose many of the same questions to students, or pare them down to support younger students in thinking about fairness/unfairness as it relates to economics, social stratification, and the distribution of wealth: ▪ How does socioeconomic status affect people's lives, particularly the lives of poor people? ▪ How are systems set up to benefit the rich and to promote capitalism at the expense of, and in ways that harm, the poor? ▪ How do we create a society, a world, where there are not stark differences between the wealthy and the poor? Is it okay for there to be a world where billionaires exist and yet there are children and families without homes?

continues

FIGURE 1.3 An Educator's Guide to Critical Theories, *continued*

THEORY	WHAT THESE THEORISTS ASK US TO CONSIDER	SELF-EXAMINATION: HOW CAN TEACHERS USE THE THEORIES AS A TOOL FOR THEIR SELF-EXAMINATION?	QUESTIONS TO INFLUENCE EDUCATIONAL PRACTICES
Queer Theory	• How can we expand, interpret, analyze, and even push against the treatment and use of gender constructs and identities within a text, in films, in the media, in our community, or in the world? • How are traditional ideas of gender identity and sexuality limited and potentially harmful? • In what ways are heteronormative ideals being upheld, particularly in ways that are harmful to people who do not identify as heterosexual? • In what ways are heteronormative ideas and beliefs privileged in society? And who is harmed by this? • How are labels and confines problematic? • How can embracing and seeing the world through the lens of queer theory make us more loving? • Why is it problematic to put people into boxes? • How do movements of resistance and activism greatly benefit from queer leaders, voices, and representation?	• Teachers can begin to ask these questions for themselves. What do you believe is "normal" or "right"? Where do these beliefs come from and how might they be limited or harmful? How much of your language and beliefs regarding gender identity and sexuality impact what and how you teach, as well as your perception of your students? • How are you creating and sustaining inclusive and antibias spaces with respect to student identity? • How can you commit to learning more about LGBTQIA+ communities and shift your practices and beliefs as a result?	Teachers can actually pose the same questions that queer theorists ask to their students: • What are the dangers in believing in the notion of "normal" or a "right" way of being? What does this even mean? More importantly, how are people harmed by this limited type of thinking? • How can we create spaces—rooted in empathy and love—where we see, learn from, and love on everyone? • How are traditional ideas of gender and sexuality limited and potentially harmful? • In what ways are heteronormative ideals being upheld, particularly in ways that are harmful to people who do not identify as heterosexual? • In what ways are heteronormative ideas and beliefs privileged in society?

PLEASE NOTE: ON LITERARY THEORIES, INCLUDING CRITICAL RACE THEORY, AMIDST THE CONTROVERSY

When I began writing this book, in late 2019, there did not exist deep resistance (as it looks and happens now) to critical race theory or to anti-racism measures in schools. The great racial "awakening" had not yet begun, and consequently, neither had the measures to stop or work against freedom practices in schools. Critical race theory, like the other theories listed in the figure, are meant to be tools to help us develop lenses that support our ability to consider and understand other people's experiences, especially their pain, in ways that we might not otherwise witness. Although critical race theory has been demonized and weaponized, I urge us to think about this tool, this mechanism of truthtelling, as one that brings us closer to collective liberation and healing. If we are not asking or considering how people are harmed on account of racism, if we are not expanding our truths in this way, then we do not move forward as a collective human entity. Bob Kim defines critical race theory in "What Critical Race Theory Is, and What It Means for Teachers" as "a school of thought that explores and critiques American history, society, and institutions of power (including government and legal systems) from a race-based perspective."[6] Critical race theory, which stems from the legal field and the work of Kimberlé Crenshaw (who also coined the term "intersectionality"), supports our work as anti-racist educators because it provides a framework, a lens to better understand what racism is, what it looks like, and how it functions on a very real level. Critical race theory positions educators to ask questions that they might not normally ask, especially if they are not Black or relegated to the margins in some way. Critical race theory moves us to a place of liberation because it shifts our understanding of racism. It points to the ways that racism is baked into institutions, systems, dialogue, human behavior, mindsets, school policies, and other ways of being. If we do not truly understand how racism works, we cannot truly undo it. The pushback against CRT and anti-racism stems from fear, the inability to tell the truth in America, especially historical truths, and desires on the part of some white people who wish to continue to be privileged on the basis of race, a construct that has very real implications for people who are not white. Critical race and other theories mentioned here should not be feared or weaponized, though movements to free and heal in this country have *always* been met with resistance, labeling or name-calling. In this case, critical race theory has been used as "the thing" to resist and work against. As English majors in college, we learned to apply critical theories, or literary criticisms, in order to deeply analyze a text and to do some analysis through various lenses. The theories listed below are used as a guide to support educators, to widen and deepen our thinking, and to ask meaningful questions.

continues

And, certainly, educators may wish to use or apply these criticisms in ways that are pared down to support deeper critical thinking with students. If this is something young people are able to do, I believe that educators can also activate the courage to do it. My ask—my very serious ask—as educators pursue this section is to think not about political labeling or leanings or about engaging in work that is "forbidden" and now highly controversial but rather to approach these theories and questions in ways that will lead to greater empathy, more compassion, and deeper justice, to liberation and to love. Let us not concern ourselves with name-calling or labeling but rather with embracing a lens, a way of engaging with the world, that allows us to think more critically and act more lovingly.

EXPAND YOUR NOTION OF TRUTH

Teachers must read, and teachers must study. Truthtelling and reading must go hand-in-hand. Teaching should be the most intellectual profession there is. Teachers have to be willing to diversify and display an openness to deepening their practice by studying other people's truths, including those of their students. To obtain a degree in this country, unfortunately, one has to be well versed in white dominant culture. Our educational system is intentionally ruthless and racist in this way. Measures of academic success are fully and completely tied to the notion and lie that white dominant culture is superior and necessary to achieve in this country. This means that many people have to bend and contort themselves under and within white dominant cultural norms in order to achieve success. Therefore, teachers have to counteract the knowledge that they have acquired. We have to study Black thinkers, especially the work and lives of Anna Julia Cooper, Audre Lorde, Ella Baker, Carter G. Woodson, Septima Clark, and W. E. B. Du Bois, for example. Educators must also deepen our understanding of educators who center liberation, such as bell hooks, Paulo Freire, Lisa Delpit, Dr. Bettina Love, Dr. Leigh Patel, and so many others. Research has to include the narratives and experiences of Indigenous people. Teachers have to be willing to identify and then to read about and position themselves as students of cultures, histories, and experiences that are both different from their own and also different from those that dominate what has been historically taught as "right." And teachers have to be willing to learn from their students. Teachers also cannot stop at reading. Action is required. Intellectualism and becoming critical have to be a way of being, a lifetime commitment for teachers, particularly teachers that are responsible for the hearts and minds of Black children. Teachers must always position themselves as learners. The learning process must be a reciprocal one; teachers must be willing to learn from their students and those around them, just as children learn, inherently, from their teachers. Teachers have to commit to intellectualism as a lifetime practice and must always be willing to ask themselves "How can I learn more about this?" and "How can I learn more about what I do not know?"

1. Begin by developing reading lists that go against white canonical texts, particularly those that dominate education, and read the works of educators and scholars of color, such as Carter G. Woodson, Bettina Love, Lisa Delpit, Gholdy Muhammad, Christopher Emdin, Clint Smith, Gloria Ladson-Billings, James Baldwin, W. E. B. Du Bois, Malcolm X, Ibram X. Kendi, Ta-Nehisi Coates, bell hooks, Angela Davis, Gloria Anzaldúa, adrienne maree brown, and Audre Lorde.

2. Think about how you will continue to learn. Research should accompany your practice. I can share what this looks like for me. When teaching new content—a book we are reading, for example—I dedicate hours of research to teach myself the historical context of the work. I want to ensure that I have background information to contextualize learning for my students.

3. Add to your models of excellent teaching. Immerse yourselves in educational publications, particularly schools of thought that promote Black liberation, womanist teachings, queer teachings, and works by other critical educators and thinkers who are people of color, specifically. Even as a Black woman, I continue to listen to, read about, and watch the content and works of other thinkers and practitioners. This might mean reading a book or an article, but it also means following critical folx on social media, watching interviews, and listening to podcasts. I am constantly thinking about ways to take in new information and how to take this new information back to my own work to deepen it. And when my thinking evolves because I have learned something new, I name that and I keep it going.

4. Engage with people who have a different perspective. I love to talk to, or honestly, listen to, debates, discussion, and discourse with people who are smarter than I am, with people whose lives are different from my own. One of my absolute favorite things to do is to share a meal with people

who see the world so vastly differently from the way that I see it. I listen
to their convictions, what pains them, and with a deeply curious mind,
I ask many, many questions. I often reach out to folx for help. I write to
people to ask for ideas and suggestions, and I allow learning and listening to be my happy place. I adopt and hold to a belief that to teach well,
and to teach critically, I must learn and listen more than I teach, speak,
or produce.

5. Travel if you can, or do it virtually. Traveling has opened my mind to
the world tremendously. Many barriers are broken down through global
travel, and much can be learned if we position ourselves as students. I
recognize the great privilege that exists in the ability to travel. As a teacher,
I found and soaked up opportunities that allowed me to travel and to
teach abroad. I designed fellowships and said yes to opportunities that
took me to Cuba, China, India, the Dominican Republic, South Africa,
Indonesia, Jordan, and many other countries throughout the Caribbean
and Europe. While there, I sat and experienced places, even when I was
teaching or leading, as a learner. I asked so many questions and captured
them through writing when I could. It was through travel that I understood, more deeply, the power of teaching anywhere and everywhere as a
mechanism for social change, for transformation and for healing.

6. Experience the world through your body. I listen to and experience the
world more increasingly through my body, as an embodied Black woman.
I will be speaking more to this in chapter 3, "Teaching as Healing," but
as a yoga teacher and great admirer and learner of Eastern and holistic
practices and approaches to healing, I am learning a great deal about the
body's ability to teach us, to convict us, and to allow us to grow. I engage
deeply in practices that allow the body to speak and to heal, which in
many ways then provides room for us to go more inward and examine
the self, which sets human beings up to take on the world more critically,
more beautifully, and more authentically.

We have to be willing to reorient our understanding of what it means to teach
and develop or sit with convictions that enable us to see teaching and liberation
as interconnected. We cannot do this, however, without a deep examination first
of the self, then of what we believe, how we feel, and that which convicts us. The
ultimate purpose of teaching, I think, is to teach and to lead children in ways that

will lead, simply, to a better world. A more just world, a free world, a world full of people who love and act on what it means to love, a world that understands that we cannot get to this place if we are unwilling to tell the truth.

HONOR TRUTHTELLERS

Finally, we must honor the role and place of truthtellers and truthtelling in schools. Truthtellers are those who work in schools who push back, reject the status quo, and ask educators to think differently about their work. Truthtellers encourage us to think more critically and uniquely about the world, especially in ways that honor justice. Truth can be convicting and hard, and those of us who seek to be comfortable in our practices rooted in wrongdoing (whether subconscious or unconscious) see truthtellers as "annoying" or "difficult." I often worked in schools where—as a truthteller—I was labeled difficult and angry (which is racist and sexist) or not easy to manage because I pushed back or asked questions. I heard, at times, that I was not being a "team player." As educators and humans, we are so accustomed to practices that are rooted in ills and isms that people who tell the truth about this harm are often deemed wrong and ostracized for disrupting the natural flow or rhythm in schools as we know it. The people who are moving against the grain are not always wrong; sometimes they are the most important folx in the space because they recognize where and how we can be better. For me, truthtelling in schools—as both a teacher and an educational leader—has looked like this:

- Questioning the presence of so many white leaders in educational spaces where they were making decisions for and about children who did not look like them
- Telling a white woman educational leader that she was being dismissive of a room full of Black women when she ignored our ideas and knowledge of Black and Latinx children
- Questioning leaders—both people of color and white people—about their practice of calling the police on a six-year-old in a school that boasted a commitment to anti-racism and social justice
- Telling a Black woman leader that her ideas and pushes against another Black woman were classist, elitist, and pointed to internalized oppression
- Questioning a Black male leader whose practices and ways of being were often, I felt, not rooted in integrity and were an abuse of power

- Questioning leaders and educators who often chose to remain silent about problematic practices and treatment
- Questioning a leader's decisions about school expansion and asking him to think about the harmful role of capitalism in an instance where students' academic success and opportunities were not at the forefront of the decision-making process

Schools can and ought to create spaces for truthtelling to live and prevail so that educators can take positions against harmful practices without feeling like their jobs are at risk. Schools can do this by doing the following:

- Selecting leaders who have integrity. Creating access and opportunities that allow multiple people and groups to select leaders, rather than small groups of like-minded, often white men or "white-minded" people of color who, despite their BIPOC identity, uphold and engage in practices that are harmful. (Once, when applying for a school leadership position, I was interviewed by two white men and a white woman in a school serving predominantly students of the Global Majority.)
- Create safety around and for truthtelling. Do not demonize and vilify people who are seeking to speak truth to power.
- Work against the existence of hierarchies in schools that reinforce paternalistic measures that make employees feel threatened or forced to be silent.
- Encourage and support heart-centered leadership.
- Celebrate leadership and wins that are not solely rooted in money or data from standardized tests. Create cultures of school environments that celebrate people for being truthful, having hard conversations, and being rooted in love.
- Hear, respect, and protect folx who are telling the truth, even if it feels challenging or uncomfortable.

QUESTIONS FOR TEACHERS TO CONSIDER

1. What are you teaching this current or upcoming school year?
2. What are some "truths" that exist within your discipline or required content? For humanities teachers, this might consist of historical truths or interpretations of truth; for English teachers, this might be concepts of truth around what constitutes "academic" or appropriate language or the types of texts students "must" read; for science teachers, this might be theories, ways of approaching hands-on learning, or studies.
3. In what ways are you able to disrupt, or perhaps expand, these notions of truth within your discipline?
4. In what ways can *you* commit to being a truthteller in your life and in your practice?
5. In what ways can you personally commit to deeper integrity?
6. Who are the truthtellers among you and how can you protect them?

CHAPTER 2

TEACHING AS ACTIVISM

I may be naive, but I believe that teaching can change the world. In my current work with teachers, I often ask them to consider the number of students they have taught over the span of their career. For some teachers, that means hundreds of students, and for others, thousands. That is power. That is influence. That is strength. In his address "A Talk to Teachers," James Baldwin reminds us that, as educators, we "must be prepared to 'go for broke.'" To move toward activism, to create a critical and activist foundation, teachers must be clear on the role of the teacher within society, within their community, and especially within the work of liberation. For many teachers, even *still*, there is great pause or an even greater disconnect that exists around their role in any form of resistance. Teaching, particularly teaching within the United States, is still a predominantly white female profession. This means that ideas of teaching are often interlaced with the ways that white women, specifically, uphold systems of oppression and perpetuate white supremacist ideals. There is a dangerous air surrounding the teaching field that says teachers should not be critical or intellectually curious, or resisters, that the field should instead be defined by passive and docile practices that allow our children to proceed through their years of schooling with a carefully constructed veil over their eyes that ultimately sustains oppression. Despite the growing numbers of Black, Indigenous, Latinx, and Asian and Pacific Islander people, the demographics of teachers and school leaders within the United States are predominantly white. There also exists mindsets among some teachers that they must take harmless, neutral stances within their classrooms or learning environments. Some educators do, in fact, believe that it is not their job to "ruffle feathers" by talking about or teaching controversial issues, that their role is simply to ensure that students learn.

Not only is this a dangerous—and quite harmful—notion, but it also poses great threats to the liberatory and transformative work that can and should happen in schools. Teachers, then, and educational leaders must reorient their stance on what it means to be an educator. To pursue teaching as a form of activism, educators are required to be clear on their purpose for being educators. We must reconcile this with the understanding that as educators, we either uphold and perpetuate systems of oppression or actively work against them. There is no in-between. A neutral stance is an oppressive stance.

When I began writing this book, we were not in the state that we are currently in. Before the murders of Breonna Taylor, George Floyd, and countless others at the hands of police during 2020—and the subsequent and necessary resistance thereafter—there were no deep and public forms of resistance to anti-racist practices and measures in school as they look and exist now. To be clear, there have always been movements to ensure truthtelling and the rightful place of Black history, which is American history, being taught in schools, but the resistance to this necessary work did not look like it does now. There were no movements, legislation, or great debate within the United States around halting anti-racist measures in schools, teaching "The 1619 Project" and other related works by Dr. Nikole Hannah-Jones, and the demonization of measures to remember and teach the truths connected to critical race theory. In the chapter on teaching and truthtelling, I wrote more about what critical race theory is, what it is not, and its role in the work of liberation in schools. Therefore, I would be remiss if I did not pause to dive more deeply into defining and expanding on what I mean by teaching as activism.

Any educator seeking to embark upon this practice should pause and consider for themselves what it means to be an activist. Activism can be defined in a number of ways, and depending on who you ask, activism can look different. For me, activism in teaching is embracing—in honor of the work and contributions of bell hooks in *Teaching to Transgress: Education as the Practice of Freedom*—the classroom as the most radical space. Teaching as activism requires that educators understand the power and privilege of our platform, our ability to influence and shape young minds, and, therefore, our ability to impact society, directly and indirectly. Teacher-activists understand that teaching is deeply political, despite mainstream media and perhaps popular perceptions around how teaching is apolitical. I share often when working with educators that schools are designed to perpetuate the aims of society within which they operate. Although educators might believe that schools exist in vacuums, separate from society, it is important that this truth be reconciled. Schools mirror society. Schools are microcosms of society. What society deems important and worthy of pursuit guides and dictates our curriculum, school culture, the selection of school leaders, the demographics of our teachers, and the allocation of resources. Teacher-activists have this awareness and recognize that because schools are political, and because teachers yield power, we have a civic and social responsibility to create and sustain a more equitable, socially just, radically humane, and healed world. It is a tall task, but it is a worthy one.

Activism in teaching means using the radical space of the classroom to equip students with the tools and skills necessary to participate in society in ways that lead to social justice, anti-racism, and healing—ultimately, liberation. Activism in teaching requires educators to embrace that educators do have an integral role in the resistance.

PLEASE NOTE: CAUTIONS AGAINST PERFORMATIVE ACTIVISM

Historically, not all forms of resistance or activism have looked the same. For many, activism brings up images and ideas around protest, particularly organizing, marching, and mobilizing, to evoke change. This is one way that teachers might engage in activism, yes, but it is also important to recognize the aspects, routines, skill sets, and tools within our practices as educators that can also be used for activism.

To be effective as teacher-activists, we have to be vigilant about the dangers of performative activism. After the specific murders of Black people by police in 2020 (we know that Black folx have long been murdered by police), protests demanding racial equity, justice, and at the very least accountability, there have been sweeping measures across the United States, certainly within schools, rooted not in long-term systemic change but in activism that is trendy or checks a box or is simply about monetary gain. It is harmful to exploit the suffering of others for monetary gain, which is why capitalism is such a threat to liberation and justice. Performative activism is incredibly dangerous because it undermines practices that lead to and sustain the necessary systemic change of hearts that we desperately need in our world to ensure the deepest forms of belonging and healing, the eradication of injustice, and ultimately, love. *Note*: This does not include the activism of, say, the civil rights movement, which needed to be broadcast so that there was a reckoning with racial violence in America.

Embracing our unique paths, purpose, and individuality can help with this. It is worthwhile for educators to consider the types of activism that make sense for your role, your skill set, your context, and your passions. This ultimately leads to long-term change.

DIVE INTO YOUR WORK AND IDENTITY AS A TEACHER-ACTIVIST

For educators seeking to engage in activist teaching, it may be helpful to start by defining activism and identifying social injustices within their school community. Think about the questions in figure 2.1. You can answer them on your own or with a trusted colleague or group.

FIGURE 2.1 Questions for Teacher-Activists: Getting Started

- What does activism mean to you?
- What does it mean to be a teacher-activist?
- What does it mean to pursue activism with your students within the classroom?
- What does social justice mean to you?
- What are some examples of social injustices?
- What are some of the social injustices that exist within your community?
- What are some of the social injustices that exist within your community that you are passionate about addressing?
- What social injustices need to be addressed because your students are most impacted by them?

Answering these questions will help you get a better sense of who you are and what you are passionate about. For example, my default as a teacher—which I learned to both appreciate and expand—was to center injustices around race, sexism, educational inequity, poverty, and classism. These were direct reflections of my experiences and identity. Although these are incredibly important to center and to raise consciousness and action around, it was equally important for me to understand how I "leaned" and to create space to understand what my students were passionate about, what plagued their communities, what affected their hearts, and what they were experiencing on account of their identities. Often, I choose to serve in educational spaces that mirror my own background and upbringing, but that is not always the case. And I cannot always assume that my lived experiences are those of my students. Beginning your work as a teacher-activist also means getting to know your students better so it's also important to think about who they are. Figures 2.1 and 2.2 are lists of questions to get you started.

FIGURE 2.2 Questions for Teacher-Activists: Getting to Know Your Students

- Who are your students?
- How do your students identify?
- Are there aspects of your students' identities that cause them to experience oppression? Multiple, intersecting forms of oppression? How? And how do you know this?
- What is the socioeconomic status of your students?
- Are you teaching predominantly white or largely affluent students? How will this impact how you center teaching for activism?

I often hear from educators who teach predominantly white, privileged students that they are unsure if liberatory practices make sense for their communities. They certainly do. Students who are the most privileged and have access to the most resources should be deeply learned in understanding the history of racism and other forms of oppression; how varying types of oppression function, exist, and persist; and how racism and other forms of oppression can be undone collectively. Educators employing activist, liberatory teaching practices in communities with students who are part of the Global Majority/marginalized communities should center students' healing, their power, their beauty, their history, their stories, their voices, their joy, and their rest *and* provide them with the tools, language, and skills necessary to work against systems of oppression, should they desire to. It is important that students of the Global Majority have the language and tools to name oppression.

SURRENDER TO QUESTIONS

I know that the task of using the classroom as a vehicle to disrupt and dismantle oppression can feel daunting. And often it is, especially in spaces that see truthtelling as a harmful or disruptive practice. Disruption is needed, however. As liberatory, anti-racist, and social justice teachers, we know and understand the dangers of silence and the role that schools can play in either disrupting or perpetuating oppression. I find hope, however, in the ability of teachers to do this very work because we, as Baldwin states, "deal with the minds and hearts of young people."[1] This great practice, however, of teaching for liberation, being anti-racist educators, and teaching for social justice begins with ourselves.

We have to be willing to sit with, understand, and unpack what we believe about the world, our students, and ourselves. Whether we recognize it or not, what we believe, pursue, ignore, dismiss, praise, or wonder about provides the foundation of our teaching and will inform or seep through it. We dictate what lives loudly in our classrooms. If we are silent about race, our students will also be, or they will have a war within themselves when they care about and understand the impact of racism. When we refuse to question, push back, and be curious, we create and sustain anti-intellectual classrooms where students will not truly understand the power of their minds. For Black students, this is deadly, going against the very nature of what we have long used to survive. Teachers—liberatory, activist teachers—must learn to question and believe in questioning.

One of my favorite professors at Spelman College in the midst of her lectures would ask a series of questions, not prompted questions that she had hidden in a lesson plan but questions, I gathered, that plagued her soul. There becomes a point in great teaching when there is a moment of surrender, moments that are not planned for, expected, or introduced, moments that we are not primed for in teacher-education programs. These are the completely human and spirit-led moments where, as an artist, our hearts, minds, and souls connect and surrender to the hearts, minds, and souls of our students. Where our intellect bows to the greater aspects of our being and we remember why we are here. There are moments, truly, when the text that we were teaching, where the question that the student posed, or where that experiment evokes in us the realization that *this* is the work, *this* is why we are here. Frederick Douglass describes this power of teaching:

> To properly teach it to enduce man's* potential and latent greatness, to discover and develop the noblest, highest and best that is in him. In view of this fact, no man whose business it is to teach should ever allow himself to feel that his mission is mean, inferior, or circumscribed. In my estimation, neither politics nor religion present to us a calling higher than this primary business of unfolding and strengthening the powers of the human soul. It is a permanent vocation. Some know the value of education, by having it. I know its value by not having it.[2]

This is the moment of questioning and the moment that teacher-activists must aspire to get to: when we begin to merge intellect and soul with the heartbeats of

---

* Noting here the lack of inclusivity in this language.

our students so that we can get them, and ourselves, to think differently about the world, and for students who are oppressed in some way, differently about themselves.

This requires that we prepare and surrender to questions like the ones in figure 2.3.

FIGURE 2.3 Questions for Teacher-Activists: Getting to Know Your Core Beliefs

- What do I believe about the world and my place within it?
- Why should education be liberatory? What is keeping teaching from being liberatory?
- For teachers and students: How can we create and sustain a learning environment where we are concerned for all people, especially those most impacted by racism, sexism, and other forms of oppression within society?
- How can teaching change the world?
- How can I contribute to making the world a better place through my instruction?
- How can I approach this content in ways that will help my students celebrate the beauty and power of others?
- How can I approach my content in ways that will open my students' hearts and my own?

SELECT AND CENTER TEXTS ROOTED IN ACTIVISM

Critical thinking, compassion, and empathy, I believe, are at the heart of activism: the ability to see the world, our environments, and our communities as places that can be better for all people, especially those who are regularly assaulted by racism. Activism, however, has to be informed. Activists have to have both a compassionate heart (which is why I address healing in this book) and a critical mind to "see" their worlds in critical ways. Some of the biggest obstacles to activism and liberation are illiteracy, blocked hearts, and ignorance. I share and teach often that an integral part of enslavement, genocide, and oppression is the presence of ignorance, disembodiment (people not being fully and wholly connected to themselves, their bodies, and the totality of their being), and illiteracy. If people are not educated, if they are not reading, if they are not thinking, then they are less likely to resist. If people are kept from connecting to all aspects of their humanity, including their bodies, their hearts (how they feel about a matter; their connection to consciousness), we are not inclined to see the humanity of others. The critical and intentional use of texts, therefore, are paramount for an activist-teacher and an activist-student. Texts are one powerful tool (there are many other tools) for educators, especially teachers.

As an English teacher, I obviously anchored my courses in texts, but I encourage all teachers and educators to consider how texts live within and guide their practice in the classroom. Not all teachers are explicitly language arts teachers, but all teachers are, in fact, literacy teachers. Or at least they can be. The professors I had as an English major understood that our liberation as Black women was tied up in what and how we studied and read, so they were careful to be intentional in what we consumed and discussed. In the same way, we have to consider the texts we are selecting or placing in front of our students for them to consume. As an English teacher, I often ask students to consider the ways that dictators came to power, how power and control were stripped from people, and the different types of dehumanizing practices that were put into place during enslavement. Particularly when teaching in spaces where all my students are Black, I create opportunities for us to draw parallels between enslavement and illiteracy. Often, students read and analyze passages from *Narrative of the Life of Frederick Douglass* to deepen their understanding of the power of reading specifically and its connection to liberation. It may seem that something like a text may be minute, but as liberatory educators, we have to know that this is false. We have to be critical, deliberate, and consistent in our choice and use of texts and what we have students do with them. Systems of oppression, particularly racism, are not small or inferior. They are deliberate, deep, consistent, and intentional, so our practice must also be.

Examine Your Own Relationship with Texts

One place to begin is to evaluate (you guessed it) your own relationship with texts, particularly critical texts. Again, we cannot become critical educators overnight. We cannot assume that we can pick up a manual and all of a sudden become educators who center liberation. In fact, most educators have been trained not to center liberation, truthtelling, anti-racism, and healing. This is a part of why there is such deep resistance to such practices. The education system, including how teachers are trained, is designed to support and sustain oppressive practices. When I consider my own journey, my body of work—as it continues to expand and evolve—it is the product of my lived experiences over time. This includes what I read and listened to as a child, the lessons instilled in me, where I attended school, my hardships, where I attended college, the friends I surround myself with, the writers and thinkers whose work I have studied and continue to study.

As you prepare to select texts for your classroom or learning environment, the questions in Figure 2.4 may be a helpful place to start.

FIGURE 2.4 Text Selection Questions

- How often do you read and gain information from text?
- From what sources do you gain the information that you consume?
- Who are your favorite authors?
- What texts were you taught to value as a child? As a student?
- What texts did you read or were required for you to read when you were preparing to become an educator? What threads exist within those texts? (All white authors? All liberatory, anti-racist? All BIPOC authors? All outdated?)
- What was the last text you read?
- What is your favorite genre?
- What are you reading and studying in order to deepen your practice as a liberatory educator?
- What is currently on your syllabus for students to read or consume, and why?

Here are some of the authors and some of their works I have read or reread that continue to shape my work as I continue to evolve in my practice as an educator and a healer. For some authors, I am listing their name only to point you to their body of work, and for others, I am highlighting specific works that have shaped my practice:

- James Baldwin, *The Fire Next Time*
- bell hooks
- Audre Lorde
- Maya Angelou
- Paulo Freire, *Pedagogy of the Oppressed*
- Carter G. Woodson, *The Mis-Education of the Negro*
- Lisa Delpit, *"Multiplication Is for White People": Raising Expectations for Other People's Children*
- Gloria Ladson-Billings, *The Dreamkeepers: Successful Teachers of African American Children*
- Michelle Alexander, *The New Jim Crow: Mass Incarceration in the Age of Colorblindness.*

- Clint Smith
- Nayyirah Waheed, *salt.*
- Bettina Love, *We Want to Do More Than Survive: Abolitionist Teaching and the Pursuit of Educational Freedom*
- Monique Couvson (formerly Morris)
- Gholdy Muhammad
- adrienne maree brown, *Emergent Strategy: Shaping Change, Changing Worlds* and *Pleasure Activism: The Politics of Feeling Good*
- Resmaa Menakem
- Alice Walker
- Toni Morrison
- Ta-Nehisi Coates

Examine Text Selection

Dr. Gholdy Muhammad, author of *Cultivating Genius: An Equity Framework for Culturally and Historically Responsive Literacy*, writes powerfully about the role and function of literacy within the literary societies of the nineteenth century: "Literacy was not just for self-enjoyment of fulfillment, it was tied to action and efforts to shape the sociopolitical landscape of a country that was founded on oppression."[3] These literary societies were composed of Black scholars who understood that their education, particularly literacy, was about more than reading for the sake of reading. Literacy was a freedom practice. Black people within these societies used literacy skills to gain knowledge, deepen their intellect, become more socially conscious, and have the language and tools to be able to advocate and resist. Black people used literacy to pursue their own freedom and healing.

My aims as an English teacher are often similar. I know from my own experiences as a student growing up in an *economically* poor environment in Columbus, Ohio (I emphasize *economically* poor because poverty is not always synonymous with complete lack; the home environment my mother created for us was rich in many ways), that my education, my ability to read, was about so much more than the skill or my getting a good grade. My sister, now a therapist, and I discuss this often about our childhood and schooling. We *knew* that reading and education was tied to our liberation and opportunities, our ability to escape the environment that many were, and are, trapped within. I often teach from that place. I understand and act on two things as a teacher: (1) When I have autonomy over my text selection, I intentionally choose and sequence texts that are rooted in the liberation of my students. When I teach in affluent school communities, I teach texts in ways that allow my students to think about collective liberation and how to be advocates and changemakers for those who do not have the same opportunities or privileges. (2) When I do not have autonomy over my text selection, I supplement the core texts with more critical texts by diverse authors or teach in ways that amplify universal themes around social injustice. I include the voices of authors and people who are not centered, and I lace these units with questions, essential questions, enduring understandings, activities, and exercises that would position my students to think, read, and write critically—even if I feel the text perpetuates problematic practices (like continuing the white literary canon).

It can be helpful to start by considering the questions in figure 2.5. The resources and learning materials we place in front of students and how we position students to engage with them are also integral parts of activist teaching.

FIGURE 2.5 Questions to Help You Examine Text Selection

- Know that there are various forms or types of texts that exist. You can incorporate books, articles, essays, magazines, videos, film, documentaries, and music into your instruction, regardless of the subject or age that you teach.
- Consider: Why are you using this text as opposed to others? If you are being mandated, how can you supplement the mandated texts?
- Whose narrative or story is the dominant one in the text?
- Is the text representative of your student body?
- Will your students find the text engaging?
- Is the text culturally responsive? Is it relevant?
- How accessible is the text?
- Whose voices are silenced within the text?
- Who is the author?
- When was the text written or created or produced?
- What is the context of the text?
- What texts can you include to support your own and students' ability to think critically? To think about liberation?
- What critical texts can you use within your discipline? What scholars, educators, or writers are you following or reading who provide strategies and produce workaround activism and critical thinking within your specific discipline or within the disciplines that you teach?

Next, consider your situation. Do you have autonomy over text selection? If not, how can you supplement the required texts in a way that helps students think critically and through an activist lens? Figures 2.6 and 2.7 show examples of text selections when I had autonomy and when I did not. Both showcase how to use texts, or supplement texts, in ways that center liberation.

FIGURE 2.6 Text Selection with Autonomy

TEXT SELECTION	WAYS I CENTERED LIBERATION AND ACTIVISM
"A Letter to My Nephew" from James Baldwin's *The Fire Next Time*	This was one of the first texts I taught in the year to communicate why I teach and what I thought was important for students to understand. I wanted students to make connections to their summer reading text, *Kindred* by Octavia Butler, and begin to examine how enslavement in the Americas had devastating ramifications. ▪ Students analyzed this text and drew connections between what Baldwin describes and the Black experience today. ▪ Students also used Baldwin's text as an example of how to use language, specifically writing, to tell the truth about the experiences of Black people in America. ▪ Students made connections between this text and Ta-Nehisi Coates's *Between the World and Me*. ▪ Students began to think about how to address these existing issues with a creative writing exercise entitled "Dear Injustice." In this exercise, students were asked to identify an injustice that they felt passionate about and to write to that injustice. ▪ We used these texts during the first week of school and often came back to them throughout the year.
"Hair," by Elizabeth Acevedo	▪ Students read a variety of texts during our poetry unit during the month of April and culminated in a poetry café. ▪ My students represented peoples of the Global Majority, which included a number of Latinx students. Students watched the spoken word performance of Acevedo's "Hair." ▪ In addition to analyzing skills such as tone, imagery, and metaphor, students analyzed and discussed topics such as: colorism and anti-Blackness in Latinx cultures and communities, attitudes and connections to enslavement, self-love and identity, identity, and language politics. ▪ Students also crafted their own poems modeled after Acevedo to advocate for issues of importance to them.
13th, by Ava DuVernay	During a unit when students were using Michelle Alexander's *The New Jim Crow: Mass Incarceration in the Age of Colorblindness* as an anchor text, students were also invited, as an additional learning opportunity, to watch DuVernay's *13th*. Students were then asked to make connections between the two texts and to what they were seeing and, perhaps, experiencing. I encouraged students to think about what they could *do* with this information and how they might apply it or use it as armor.

FIGURE 2.6 Text Selection with Autonomy, *continued*

TEXT SELECTION	WAYS I CENTERED LIBERATION AND ACTIVISM
Poetry of Resistance: Voices for Social Justice by Francisco X. Alarcón and Odilia Galván Rodríguez	• Students read poems by Gwendolyn Brooks as well as Langston Hughes, Claude McKay, and a number of other Harlem Renaissance poets. I also invited a world-renowned poet to work with students on crafting their narratives through poetry. • Students analyzed, compared, and used as mentor texts selections from *Poetry of Resistance: Voices for Social Justice*. I chose this text because it centers the activism and voices of Latinx students in Arizona who resisted and displayed acts of civil disobedience against Arizona's SB 1070 legislation. I wanted to center student protest and activism so my students would not feel as though their age disqualified them from activism. • Students crafted poems, including spoken word performances, around issues such as police brutality, homophobia, gentrification in Harlem, and an overwhelming white leadership in their charter school network.
"Universal Declaration of Human Rights"	During our rhetoric unit, where students examined and studied a wide range of texts, including advertisements, commercials, political and historical speeches, poems, and essays, I wanted to provide a deeper foundation for students to think about everything through the lens of social justice and human rights. Students analyzed, rewrote, and created visual representations of the "Universal Declaration of Human Rights." Once students demonstrated their understanding of this text, they were asked to apply their knowledge and use the language of the rights to both identify and work against human rights violations. This unit culminated in students creating their own rhetoric campaigns. They worked in groups or pairs on issues of importance to them. Students were asked to engage social media and use rhetorical strategies to advocate for or resist against issues that were most important to them. Students addressed issues such as bullying, rape culture, police brutality, homophobia, gentrification, racism, sexism, colorism, and white standards of beauty.

Figure 2.6 demonstrates some of the types of texts I chose when I had complete autonomy over my curriculum and demonstrates how the texts varied based on where I was teaching and the identities of my students. The next figure will show how I have centered liberatory teaching practices through the types of exercises, practices, or the type of work I engaged students in when the texts were required or preassigned. In some cases, I also supplemented texts when I did not have autonomy over required texts. I think it is important for teachers to see that liberatory pedagogy can be employed regardless of where you are teaching.

FIGURE 2.7 Required Texts and How I Have Taught Them Through a Liberatory Lens

REQUIRED TEXTS	HOW I SUPPLEMENT REQUIRED TEXTS AND TEACH THROUGH AN ACTIVIST LENS
The Crucible, by Arthur Miller	• Students explored and researched examples of modern-day witch hunts. • Students explored Tituba's character (an often highly overlooked and disregarded character), racism, and how her character is portrayed and situated within a text with mainly white characters.
Night, by Elie Wiesel	This is already an incredibly powerful text and when teaching this text in an affluent school, I wanted students to dive more deeply into human behavior and to consider—truly through all the texts we explored—how the study of history and specifically the Holocaust has implications on how we ought to act and be in the best interest of humanity today. In addition to studying the Holocaust, students researched other types of genocide and were able to pull out, analyze, discuss, and reflect on themes and patterns around human behavior, harm, oppression, silencing, and erasure that existed across various types of genocide. Students examined the ways Adolf Hitler came to power and the connections between dictatorships and censorship. Students were able to grapple with powerful themes around how censorship, specifically, and controlling educational outcomes can and have been used to perpetuate harm and violence against groups of people. In addition to reading *Night*, students read and analyzed the poetry of children who were in concentration camps. Students read texts about the bystander effect and the dangers of silence. *Night* was a central text that we used to draw connections between intellect, education, compassion, empathy, action and activism.
Macbeth, by William Shakespeare	Students zoned in on Lady Macbeth's character, as well as the other women characters in the text. They grappled with themes around the characterization, particularly the demonization of powerful women. Students read mainly supplementary articles and, in some cases, watched videos to amplify these ideas. Students explored the psychology of human behavior. They also read additional texts about greed and power.

One of my favorite books of poetry, *salt.*, by Nayyirah Waheed, addresses the importance of centering the stories, histories, and texts by people of color. She describes this as the correct order of learning. Figure 2.8 lists some of the texts I have used as an English language arts teacher to achieve this goal of centering the stories, histories, and experiences of people of the Global Majority through liberatory text selection. Many of these texts make it into my syllabus no matter where I teach and whether I am teaching young people or adults.

FIGURE 2.8 My Go-To Teaching Texts to Center Liberation

- *The Fire Next Time*, James Baldwin
- *13th*, Ava DuVernay
- *The Combahee River Collective Statement*
- Poetry from *The Collected Works of Langston Hughes*
- *For Colored Girls Who Have Considered Suicide When the Rainbow Is Enuf*, Ntozake Shange
- *Lemonade*, Beyoncé
- *In the Time of the Butterflies*, Julia Alvarez
- *Kindred*, Octavia Butler
- Spoken word and poems by Elizabeth Acevedo, such as "Hair" and "Afro-Latina"
- *Teaching My Mother How to Give Birth*, Warsan Shire
- *salt.*, Nayyirah Waheed
- *The House on Mango Street*, Sandra Cisneros
- *Things Fall Apart*, Chinua Achebe
- "Keep Ya Head Up," Tupac
- *To Pimp a Butterfly*, Kendrick Lamar
- *We Should All Be Feminists*, Chimamanda Ngozi Adichie

DESIGN UNITS WITH LIBERATION IN MIND

Over the span of my teaching career, I have had to balance the fullness of my personal life, my experiences, my trauma, with the demands that come with teaching and loving students. A part of this included grappling with teaching students while they were dealing with some of the very real and harsh realities that come with being a Black person in America. Most of my students were reading significantly below grade level and many had experienced significant trauma. Some students were battling depression, had family members with terminal cancer, or had parents who were incarcerated; others were experiencing homelessness, juggling school and jobs to provide for their families, going through the foster care system, and grieving family members.

Not only did my teaching have to be critical; it also had to be deeply humanistic, relevant, and rooted in love, healing, care, and hope. And I never feel like I got it right. It is nearly impossible for teachers within our current school systems to do what is most needed for our students. My students, rightfully, did not prioritize writing essays. Many of them tried, however. They understood that education was a gateway, but they also were living with and experiencing the shackles of poverty, injustice, racism, sexism, and every other intentionally designed structure there to hold them back. Still, many of my students showed up each day, and I had to work through engaging them, teaching them the skills they needed to at least try to play a part in this system. Despite many of their awful and unfair circumstances, I wanted them to enjoy and to take part in what they were learning. I wanted to create opportunities within the learning, writing, creating, sharing, and critiquing for them to have space, to breathe—even if only for the fifty minutes that they had my class each day.

Take, for example, a unit of study I designed and created for a high school English literature class. Many of my students were well below grade level (which points more to systemic oppression and its impact on literacy rates than their ability and will) and still needed to pass the state standardized exam. But for me, I understood that was not what was most important for my students. Before leaving high school, I wanted them to have tools that would allow them to develop a critical reading of their worlds. I wanted them to be able to have the language so that they could explain their oppression and understand how to combat it. I needed students to feel seen and heard, and I wanted to reinforce that they were beautiful, worthy, and powerful. So I designed a lesson—beginning with all the endings in mind for my students.

Backward design in unit planning is a strong tool and a practice that social justice educators must develop. It is important to think through and understand where you want students to land at the end of a unit. Certainly, teachers are bound in many respects to teaching the skills, content, and standards tied to the grade levels they are teaching, but we cannot end there. I often tell educators to think of the standards or exams as the baseline, not the end goal. One of the largest misconceptions or challenges that I run into when teaching teachers how to teach critically—how to engage anti-racist practices in their instruction or how to teach for social justice—is how to get around the pressure of the standards and tests that we must teach. It is an understandable frustration. It is important to note that teachers can use and do it all. True liberation would mean eradicating systems and measures that are rooted in racism, but just like when I was teaching, I realized the urgency of now because the system and our world simply were not there yet, so I had to teach critically and creatively.

I start with a unit planning template, like the one in figure 2.9. The unit plan is one of my favorite parts of curriculum design. This is where we can play, create art, and expand our thinking about where to go with a unit. The unit plan should extend directly from the scope and sequence; it allows us to narrow the focus into one specific body of work.

The unit plan is where we can show that teaching standards (which we might often feel restricted by) and teaching for activism, teaching for healing, and teaching for love—essentially liberatory teaching—do not have to be mutually exclusive. It includes guiding questions for teachers to consider when designing their own unit or planning to teach one that has already been designed.

I often have this conversation with academic leaders in schools about whether teachers should be designing their own curriculum, or if it is okay for teachers to use something that has already been designed. My personal and professional opinion—though I know this is layered—is that in order to be truly culturally responsive, teachers need to be able to employ the skill sets and tools to design a curriculum that most responds to the needs of the students in front of them. The reality of our school system today, however, is that teachers do not always enter schools with the skills necessary to adequately plan for their students, which is a much bigger economic and political issue. Liberatory teaching is best employed by educators who are skilled in both content knowledge and pedagogical practices, and who understand what it means to center liberation. In order to ensure this happens in schools, we need an education system that values teachers, that pays teachers what they are worth, that has school hours and demands that are appropriate for any human being, and that offers teacher education programs that are rooted in anti-racism, liberation, and healing. School systems and leaders have much work to do to get there. In the meantime, we are able to use the tools at our disposal, like engaging with our unit plans and other planning tools in ways that can set us up to center liberatory practices.

FIGURE 2.9 Unit Planning Template

UNIT INFO

Title:
Grade:
Subject:
Unit Duration:

UNIT OVERVIEW

- *What do you plan to accomplish with your students through this unit of study?*
- *What are your goals for your students?*
- *Why do you want students to engage in this content? What critical knowledge, understanding, and skills do you want students to leave this unit of study with? How can you and your students contribute to making the world a better place through this unit of study?*

ESSENTIAL QUESTIONS

What are the critical questions that will guide teaching and learning for this unit of study or for the year? What questions can you pose to students that will guide students in thinking about how to make the world a better place and how to take critical action?

ENDURING UNDERSTANDINGS

What learning do you want students to gain from this unit that they will be able to use and come back to beyond this unit? What is the learning that you want to last? What do you want students to understand about the world, society, their communities, and themselves through engaging in this unit? How are you able to make connections between the content explored in the unit and activism?

FIGURE 2.9 Unit Planning Template, *continued*

FINAL OUTPUTS
What are the final demonstrations of learning that students will produce (e.g., essays, speeches, projects, debates, and seminars)?

STANDARDS
What are the standards that are tied to your course that you will have to teach to or include in this unit of study?

CORE TEXTS	SUPPLEMENTARY TEXTS
What are the anchor texts that you will or in some cases must teach?	*How can you diversify and offer texts to supplement the core texts? Texts can be art forms, music, advertisements, images, films, documentaries, articles, letters, videos, and podcasts.*

KEY TERMINOLOGY
What new terms will students need to know to have access to the content you will teach during this unit?

continues

FIGURE 2.9 Unit Planning Template, *continued*

KNOWLEDGE	SKILLS
What will students need to know? What will students know as a result of participating in this unit?	*What will students learn to do, in terms of academic skill)? Refer to the verbs in Bloom's taxonomy.*
SUMMATIVE ASSESSMENTS	FORMATIVE ASSESSMENTS

Figure 2.10 is an example of how I used the planning template for a class of seniors who were learning about literary criticisms and the media.

As I mentioned earlier, when I began writing this book, and when I employed this unit of study with my students who were in the twelfth grade at the time, literary criticisms and theories, such as critical race theory, were not being weaponized or banned at the time. They had their rightful place within the academy and within some classrooms with educators who chose to uplift them. Even if they had been weaponized or banned, I still would have engaged in a unit of study like this because of its impact with and for my students. What we often fail to realize is that in efforts that ban books or the teaching of Black history are the lived realities and the harm that is inflicted on students and people whose histories are silenced and those who are relegated to the margins of society. Efforts and legislation to ban truthtelling—further perpetuating oppression and erasure—do not truly see or care for people, or for the young people we serve who need to learn about their history. In studying queer theory, critical race theory, and feminist theory—which can be pared down for students to access in ways that are appropriate and at their level—my students felt seen and heard. They felt like they had the language and tools to critique the oppression they were experiencing but that they did not necessarily have the language for.

FIGURE 2.10 Example of Unit Planning

A UNIT PLANNING TEMPLATE

UNIT INFO
Title: Literary Criticisms and the Media
Grade: 12
Subject: English Literature
Unit Duration: 4–6 Weeks

UNIT OVERVIEW
What do you plan to accomplish with your students through this unit of study?
What are your goals for your students?
Why do you want students to engage in this content? What critical knowledge, understanding, and skills do you want students to leave this unit of study with? How can you and your students contribute to making the world a better place through this unit of study?

Over the course of this unit, I want my students to engage critically with the media. (1) I want students to dive into literary criticisms, particularly feminist theory, Marxist theory, critical race theory, and queer theory, so that they are able to understand sexism, racism, classism, and homophobia. (2) I also want students to be able to develop the language to discuss the forms of oppression and the lenses to be able to notice and unpack these forms of oppression. (3) I want students to feel equipped to do something about existing forms of oppression by applying literary criticisms to media forms that they interact with daily.

For students to understand the concept of rights and to become familiar with the "Universal Declaration of Human Rights," I will create this as a fifth form of literary criticism that they will use to think critically about the world and the media.

For students to be engaged, for their final demonstrations of learning, I will allow them to choose the media forms that are of interest to them. It is also important students feel that they have ownership over their learning and are able to participate in it.

I want this unit to feel real, relevant, and tangible to students so they feel inclined to participate as disruptors and interrupters of injustice. Because I am teaching Black and Brown students, I want them to be able to understand how to navigate the forms of oppression they experience daily.

ESSENTIAL QUESTIONS
What are the critical questions that will guide teaching and learning for this unit of study or for the year? What questions can you pose to students that will guide students in thinking about how to make the world a better place? How to take critical action?

- How can I engage critically with the world?
- How can I use literary criticism theories to unpack systems of oppression?
- How can I use literary criticism theories to critique messages that are promoted within popular forms of media?
- How can literature be used as a tool of resistance?

continues

FIGURE 2.10 Example of Unit Planning, *continued*

<table>
<tr><td colspan="1">

ENDURING UNDERSTANDINGS

What learning do you want students to gain from this unit that they will be able to use and come back to beyond this unit? What is the learning that you want to last? What do you want students to understand about the world, society, their communities, and themselves through engaging in this unit? How are you able to make connections between the content explored in the unit and activism?
</td></tr>
<tr><td>

- Students will be able to develop deeper critical lenses that allow them to name and critique varying forms of oppression.
- Students will develop critical lenses (through studying and applying literary criticisms) that allow them to critique and dissect messages found within varying forms of media (music, art, television, film, documentaries, etc.).
- Students will be able to unpack the messages, mindsets, and beliefs, particularly those rooted in or designed to sustain oppression found in various media forms.
</td></tr>
<tr><td>

FINAL OUTPUTS

What are the final demonstrations of learning that students will produce (e.g., essays, speeches, projects, debates, and seminars)?
</td></tr>
<tr><td>

- Final presentations on media subject of their choosing
- Mini-essays
- Film literary analysis essay
- Teaching the class about literary theories (small groups or pairs)
</td></tr>
<tr><td>

STANDARDS

What are the standards that are tied to your course that you will have to teach to or include in this unit of study?
</td></tr>
<tr><td>

CCSS.ELA-LITERACY.RL.11–12.1: Cite strong and thorough textual evidence to support analysis of what the text says explicitly as well as inferences drawn from the text, including determining where the text leaves matters uncertain.

CCSS.ELA-LITERACY.RL.11–12.2: Determine two or more themes or central ideas of a text and analyze their development over the course of the text, including how they interact and build on one another to produce a complex account; provide an objective summary of the text.

CCSS.ELA-LITERACY.RL.11–12.3: Analyze the impact of the author's choices regarding how to develop and relate elements of a story or drama (e.g., where a story is set, how the action is ordered, how the characters are introduced and developed).

CCSS.ELA-LITERACY.RL.11–12.4: Determine the meaning of words and phrases as they are used in the text, including figurative and connotative meanings; analyze the impact of specific word choices on meaning and tone, including words with multiple meanings or language that is particularly fresh, engaging, or beautiful. (Include Shakespeare as well as other authors.)

CCSS.ELA-LITERACY.RL.11–12.5: Analyze how an author's choices concerning how to structure specific parts of a text (e.g., the choice of where to begin or end a story, the choice to provide a comedic or tragic resolution) contribute to its overall structure and meaning as well as its aesthetic impact.
</td></tr>
</table>

FIGURE 2.10 Example of Unit Planning, *continued*

CCSS.ELA-LITERACY.RL.11–12.6: Analyze a case in which grasping a point of view requires distinguishing what is directly stated in a text from what is really meant (e.g., satire, sarcasm, irony, or understatement).

CCSS.ELA-LITERACY.W.11–12.1: Write arguments to support claims in an analysis of substantive topics or texts, using valid reasoning and relevant and sufficient evidence.

CCSS.ELA-LITERACY.W.11–12.2: Write informative/explanatory texts to examine and convey complex ideas, concepts, and information clearly and accurately through the effective selection, organization, and analysis of content.

CCSS.ELA-LITERACY.W.11–12.4: Produce clear and coherent writing in which the development, organization, and style are appropriate to task, purpose, and audience. (Grade-specific expectations for writing types are defined in standards 1–3 above.)

CCSS.ELA-LITERACY.W.11–12.5: Develop and strengthen writing as needed by planning, revising, editing, rewriting, or trying a new approach, focusing on addressing what is most significant for a specific purpose and audience. (Editing for conventions should demonstrate command of Language standards 1–3 up to and including grades 11–12 here.)

CCSS.ELA-LITERACY.W.11–12.6: Use technology, including the Internet, to produce, publish, and update individual or shared writing products in response to ongoing feedback, including new arguments or information.

CORE TEXTS	SUPPLEMENTARY TEXTS
We Should All Be Feminists, Chimamanda Ngozi Adichie	"Flawless," Beyoncé (song)
Excerpts from *The Combahee River Collective Statement*	*Half the Sky* (documentary)
The New Jim Crow: Mass Incarceration in the Age of Colorblindness, Michelle Alexander	*The Crips and Bloods: Made in America* (documentary)
"Universal Declaration of Human Rights"	Excerpts from *Scandal* (TV series)
Select articles by Kimberlé Crenshaw	Excerpts from *Mean Girls* (film)
Select articles by bell hooks	Multiple essays and articles on various critical theories
Select articles and essays on queer theory	*Mulan* (film)
Select articles and essays on Marxist theory	Students chose a variety of media forms for their analysis, presentations, and essays:
	• *Time: The Kalief Browder Story* (documentary series)
	• *Love and Hip Hop* (TV series)
	• *Empire* (TV series)
	• *Being Mary Jane* (TV series)
	• *Divergent* (film)
	• J. Cole songs/lyrics
	• *Bad Girls Club* (TV series)

continues

FIGURE 2.10 Example of Unit Planning, *continued*

KEY TERMINOLOGY
What are the terms or key phrases that will be integral to students' ability to demonstrate knowledge of the content explored in this unit? What terminology will you need to front-load?

• Critical race theory	• Race and racism
• Queer theory	• Social construct
• Feminist	• Queer
• Feminist theory	• Marxist
• Womanist	• Marxist theory

KNOWLEDGE	SKILLS
What will students need to know? What will students know as a result of participating in this unit?	*What will students learn to do, in terms of academic skills? Refer to the verbs in Bloom's taxonomy.*
• Students will be able to develop deeper critical lenses that allow them to name and critique varying forms of oppression. • Students will develop critical lenses (through studying and applying literary criticisms) that allow them to critique and dissect messages found within varying forms of media (music, art, television, film, documentaries, etc.). • Students will be able to explore the relationship between developing critical lenses through which they can analyze and critique the world and action or activism. • Students will be able to unpack the messages, mindsets, and beliefs, particularly those rooted in or designed to sustain oppression found in various media forms.	• Students will be able to define select literary criticisms. • Students will be able to apply literacy criticisms to various texts and media forms. • Students will be able to name, identify, and unpack forms of oppression, such as racism, sexism, classism, and homophobia, using literary criticisms. • Students will be able to craft analytical essays. • Students will be able to conduct research and synthesize information from varying texts.

SUMMATIVE ASSESSMENTS	FORMATIVE ASSESSMENTS
• Essays whereby students apply two or three literary criticisms explored in the unit to a media form of their choice. • Creative in-class presentations whereby students apply two or three literary criticisms explored in the unit to a media form of their choice.	• Students practice applying literary criticisms as they learn them to varying media forms including clips from the TV series *Scandal* and the films *Mean Girls* and *Mulan*. • Students conduct in-class research and write shared definitions and questions about each literary criticism explored in the unit. • Students write short responses demonstrating their ability to apply literary criticism to texts.

Standards from National Governors Association Center for Best Practices, Council of Chief State School Officers (2010).

This helped my students to be able to name, identify, and feel seen and heard, and they felt that they were being pushed academically and prepared for new academic heights. The reality of why work like this is being banned is because we live in a country and climate now—as we always have—that does not want young people, especially Black people and those who are relegated to the margins, to have the tools to end the oppression they are experiencing. To mitigate it. To work against it. This unit remains in this text because it is one of the most powerful that I was able to teach. Students not only felt that they were able to tap into their power; they felt joy and excitement in being able to apply literary criticism to various forms of media that they consumed. I understand that for some this will feel controversial. The role of the educator is not to tell students what to think but to guide them in ways, and to provide learning opportunities and tools, that create space for critical, radical, and imaginative thinking. This is just one example of the type of lesson I used to amplify liberatory teaching.

DISPELLING SOME MYTHS AROUND TEACHING AS ACTIVISM

MYTH 1: YOUNG STUDENTS CANNOT DO THIS WORK. This is not true. All students and all ages benefit from activist-centered teaching. This is where we have to begin to think about our work differently as educators. There are developmentally appropriate ways to engage students in liberatory work. I share often when working with educators that even two-year-olds know when something seems "unfair." It is important, too, for educators to know that some core skills and principles that are developed with younger students, such as communication, compassion, empathy, identity, and self-advocacy, lay the foundational blocks that ultimately lead to justice.

MYTH 2: ACTIVIST, LIBERATORY TEACHING CAN ONLY BE DONE WITHIN THE HUMANITIES. This is not true. Teachers of *all* disciplines can draw powerful and enduring connections between their content and justice-oriented work. Although the humanities focus on people and the issues that exist within humanity, there exists powerful correlations between numbers, statistics, and economic injustice, for example.

- In math, you can build great problem-solving skills with students. The analysis of graphs and charts can reveal and explain injustices and disparities.

continues

- In the sciences, students can devise and design solutions for social issues, such as global warming and the mistreatment of animals. Biology can be tied matters and examples of deep historical racism. Students can learn about Henrietta Lacks and the Tuskegee experiment, as well as the powerful inventions of BIPOC people, who have created a better world for students.
- Through the study of world languages, students can explore themes of language, power, injustice, colonization, enslavement, and racism *and* explore the beauty of culture, the richness of Indigenous culture, and engage in assignments around reclamation.
- Through health and physical education, students can explore healing and wellness as resistance and as practices of self-care and joy.
- Through the arts, students can explore how the arts have been central to activism and movements of resistance. Students can examine and explore critical and joyful messages through contemporary or culturally responsive music and artists. (I often taught Beyonce's work, as well as other artists in order to do this.)

MYTH 3: IF I DO NOT HAVE AUTONOMY OVER MY CURRICULUM, I CANNOT ENGAGE IN LIBERATORY PRACTICES. I believe that teacher autonomy and true culturally responsive education walk hand-in-hand. Although I know there are many teachers who do not or cannot have autonomy, I believe the most effective teachers are those who have been well prepared, are experts in both their content and pedagogical practices, and who have a firm understanding of their students. Critical, liberatory pedagogy requires all of this. However, some teachers are bound by a prescribed curriculum. But educators can add on to the curriculum, design critical essential questions that guide the learning, and provide supplementary materials that are rooted in equity and justice. Teachers can also design learning outputs, learning processes or demonstrations of learning such as projects (project-based learning is a powerful liberatory tool), essays that respond to questions that raise students' consciousness, showcases, learning exhibitions, plays, skits, artwork, dance, speeches, and experiments. Pursue opportunities that invite students to apply and show what they know.

QUESTIONS FOR TEACHERS TO CONSIDER

1. What is your definition of activism?
2. How can you center activism through your teaching?
3. What pressing social injustices are your students facing? How will you utilize your platform as a teacher to work against these issues?
4. What support will you need?
5. What are you most excited about in centering activism through your teaching?

CHAPTER 3

TEACHING AS HEALING

I am absolutely fascinated and taken by the work of healers. Healers such as medical doctors that are referenced in the West and certainly the ancient healing modalities and practitioners that are found East, in African cultures, and within Indian, Chinese, Balinese, and Japanese cultures. I have found it a privilege and an honor to cultivate and hold healing spaces that are rooted in some of these traditions, such as yoga, meditation, mindfulness, Reiki, other forms of energy healing, dance, and even therapy or journaling. I am moved by and have experienced the power within the healing arts. The ability, certainly, to feel better, and the power of being seen, felt, heard, and, at times, held. The power of understanding and knowing that energy can be transformed, that pain does not have to always exist, and most importantly, that I am most connected to other beings when I am at complete peace and healed within myself.

But what does healing have to do with teaching?

Often in practices that bring us closer to liberation, there is great emphasis on upending structures and systems—inequitable structures, systems of oppression. There has to be an understanding that systems and structures are both created and sustained by people. *We* are doing this. *We* must undo them. There is a great deal of harm that societies—people—either directly or indirectly have done to the marginalized within a respective society. In America specifically, there is a great deal of intentional harm inflicted upon generations of Black people and, ultimately, Black children. If we are to create transformative schools that are rooted in liberation, freedom, joy, and belonging, what I imagine are the qualities that any successful society desires to have for its children, schools must concern themselves with the healing and well-being of children and the well-being of the adults who serve them.

We must be vigilant about the ways as Ta-Nehisi Coates explains "that racism is a visceral experience, that it dislodges brains, blocks airways, rips muscle, extracts organs, cracks bones, breaks teeth."[1] And, if this is to be done effectively, educators must be willing to examine the ways that Black lives specifically are harmed and therefore how some of this harm can be healed within schools.

To be clear, I am not saying that the healing of children must only center on or emphasize the healing of Black lives. My context, my reference point, and my experience are rooted in Blackness, and especially in Black womanhood—so this is the pain I recognize first. I, too, must do my part to extend beyond my lived experience to understand others' experiences and pain. To be healed, to be whole, for any society to thrive and be well, it helps to pursue this work through an intersectional lens. The Black movements of resistance in America, for example, are a helpful place for educators to start—though it is not the only place to start—particularly the recent movements of resistance, as they call for a consideration of *everyone* who is marginalized, and the ways that Black folx who sit at the intersection of multiple forms of oppression—Black, poor, and trans women and girls are uniquely harmed. The current movements of resistance, particularly those that honor intersectionality, require that efforts made in the name of liberation and in creating a better society must be inclusive of all who are harmed, brutalized, and marginalized. Black people, the poor, Indigenous people, Asian American people, Latinx people, women and girls, particularly girls of color, communities that are harmed due to homophobia and transphobia, those who are harmed on account of xenophobia, language, indifference, hate, or other forms of bigotry. We must consider all of it—all of the harm and all of the wrongdoing—if we are to progress as a society. It is hypocritical, I think and often share, to focus on one ism or phobia and negate the others that exist. We get nowhere that way, and the harm is perpetuated. These ideas, however, are not meant to conflate the harmful arguments often levied against movements that seek to end racial violence specifically. I want to be clear that "all lives matter" rhetoric in response to movements to protect and preserve Black lives are forms of gaslighting, are reductive, and overlook the experiences and harm that Black folx have long endured in the US and in the greater African diaspora.

Like teaching as activism, teaching as healing asks educators to think about our roles differently, through a lens of empathy and of action. Teaching as healing requires educators to grapple with and serve students from a place of understanding that students are not broken, but that many students, particularly Black students, are forced to labor within and under systems ultimately created to destroy them.

Baldwin reminds us of this in "A Letter to My Nephew": "This innocent country set you down in a ghetto in which, in fact, it intended that you should perish."[2] Racism and harm against BIPOC communities, especially Black people across the African diaspora and within the United States, have long been intentional and deliberate. Therefore, our efforts to eradicate harm—to sustain equity, justice, and liberation—must, too, be intentional and deliberate. Embracing teaching as a healing practice can support this.

Healing is a powerful practice because (1) it is deeply humanistic and allows us to return to the human aspect of our practice as educators; (2) it is concerned with repairing harm, with restoration; and (3) it requires us to deal not with the symptoms but with the roots of an issue. Healing is radical in this sense. This is an approach we desperately need in a profession that centers our children.

When I consider why a healing ethos is needed in our practice as educators, I am quickly reminded of the harm, the pain, the emphasis that needs to be placed on truly *seeing* people, on seeing young people. I believe that a healing ethos in education is a powerful one because it allows us to deal with the ways in which we all may be hurting, where we need to heal and be more human, the places where we can afford to be softer. It is *that* place, that place of humanity, of being, of belonging, of sitting, and of caring with self, that compels us to be the most powerful and effective humans. When I consider the ills in the world that are created and sustained by people, and people who create systems to sustain such harm, I think about the ways in which humanity has departed from a place of wholeness and how a part of the repair is to restore, to reconcile. When I teach, talk, and write about isms and phobias (the harm), I speak of them as the ills in the world. I believe that fear, brokenness, the lack of self-love, and a disconnect with and from spirit/creator/God is what causes us to harm one another and ourselves. A healing ethos allows us to unpack and understand systems of oppression, racism, bigotry, and other forms of harm at a visceral level. To move toward liberation, healing is absolutely a part of what we need.

Racism and other forms of intersectional oppression are brutal. Psychological harm, mental harm, spiritual harm, physical harm, and emotional harm stemming from racism all exist in our schools. Centering healing in teaching, centering care in teaching, allows us to ensure that our students are afforded the full range of their humanity and experience. Without a holistic pursuit toward liberation, we fail to completely and adequately serve our students.

I think the debate around anti-racism, critical race theory, and teaching texts such as "The 1619 Project" stems from a few places. The first is America's difficult relationship with truthtelling, the inability to recognize wrongdoing in an effort to sustain it. The second, and what I hope to address in this chapter, is that there is a profound lack of understanding around the ways that racism, patriarchy, and other phobias and isms are hurtful.

I urge educators and adults who serve young people to consider, sit with, and then do something about the pain, the trauma that is inflicted onto the body, psyche, and spirit as a result of racism. Racism breaks people; racism breaks the spirit; racism actually hurts. We have to move away from thinking about racism and patriarchy and other forms of social injustice as mere theories, as only systems, injustices, and practices that seem far removed from people, from the human experience. Healing requires grounding, truthtelling, and dealing with matters and harm in ways that are deeply humanistic. Outside of being sustained through systems, practices, institutions, interpersonal actions, dialogue, and internalization, racism and patriarchy are sustained when we remove such systems and practices from being, from *our* ways of being. People do harm. People create systems and structures, laws, and policies that sustain harm. People have to, therefore, engage in the practices that lead to healing. As educators, we have a social and civic responsibility to ensure that *all* students are well.

I want educators to process the following:

- Racism hurts.
- Racism makes people feel and believe that they are not beautiful.
- Capitalism and poverty can make people feel invisible.
- People die—people actually die—due to racism.
- Patriarchy reduces women to ideological roles and makes women and girls feel as though they cannot fully be themselves.
- Women and girls are killed because of toxic masculinity and patriarchal ideas.
- Poor Black women and girls suffer from multiple and simultaneous forms of oppression, such as racism, sexism, and poverty, which deeply assaults their humanity and right to be.

Racism, patriarchy, homophobia, and transphobia are not merely words or fabricated ideas in the name of dividing nations; they are systems, practices, beliefs, and ideals that are created and sustained by humans, and they cause insufferable harm.

Raising consciousness about, undoing, and mitigating harm are a part of the work of all human beings, particularly educators.

UNDERSTAND HOW SCHOOLS HARM STUDENTS

Schools do harm. Some educators might question why healing ought to be a part of our field, our practice. It is important to acknowledge and understand the ways that schools are sites of pain for many students. Schools—particularly schools in the United States—are institutions that are built upon and designed to sustain white supremacy culture. A white supremacist culture is predicated upon the suffering of those who are not white. This means that nonwhite cultures are often erased, dismissed, minimized, exoticized, trivialized, demonized, or excluded altogether. A part of an educator's job—at the most basic level—is to ensure that students are well, that our children are in spaces where they feel and know that they belong, that students' safety is ensured, and that students are able to learn. Racism, sexism, capitalism, and other forms of oppression that exist within our world and society prohibit many students' ability to belong, to feel safe, and, ultimately, to learn. Culturally responsive practitioners and scholars, for example, drive home the necessity of including students' cultures and ways of being as foundational to their ability to belong, be, and learn. Many schools fail at this. Therefore, I submit, for educators' thinking, being, and practice, a way of engaging with students and with this deeply humanistic practice in ways that will lead to students' overall success and wholeness. We have to first understand how schools harm and what we can do to ensure our students' healing.

Anti-racism, social justice, and activism in teaching are not about dividing the nation or about making people feel bad; *it is about healing and truthtelling.* Our world, our human actions, have a way of making some people feel half full. What does it look like to create more space for empathy and integrity within our field as educators? What if we dared to consider the ways that our profession uniquely positions us to play a role in healing, in repairing the harm that systems of oppression have inflicted upon Black bodies specifically?

Educators who are seeking to cultivate liberatory spaces for children and young people—particularly Black children and children from any community that is relegated to the margins of any society—have to first be willing to grapple with what it means to be an educator. For some, working as an educator is a job, a task, an important one, but one that begins in the morning and ends at the close of the school day. Then there are other educators who know, believe, and operate out of the place that education, specifically to teach, is a calling. It is an art form. It is a vocation larger than oneself that requires being in tune with the larger aspects of their lives, a connection to soul, spirit, and purpose to effectively engage in the work. Still, for others, education, the classroom or learning space, is a place where educators merely teach the content. Those people feel that the learning space is one where controversial issues or topics should not enter. Educators who are working toward liberation, however, understand that education, true education, is so much more.

To fully understand the ways that schools can be places of harm, it is important to consider our practices through an intersectional lens. Kimberlé Crenshaw, a critical race theory and legal scholar, coined "intersectionality." In a 2020 article for *Time* magazine, she offers clarity about the term, what it is and what it is not in relation to the backlash against anti-racist efforts: "It's basically a lens, a prism, for seeing the way in which various forms of inequality often operate together and exacerbate each other."

Intersectionality, essentially, allows us to understand how an individual's experience can be impacted by multiple and compounding forms of oppression. For example, Black women experience oppression due to both racism and sexism. An intersectional lens is integral to liberation because it allows educators to understand and work toward the justice and freedom of those, such as Black girls, whose intersectional identities cause them to be uniquely harmed. I am intentional about using an example of Black girls because of the type of intersectional harm Black girls experience. This is another example of how thinking about the ways in which one specific group of students is harmed can lead to connections and deeper understandings of the way other groups of students may be harmed. Also, when we concern ourselves with Black women's and girls' liberation—given all of the intersections of harm and oppression we experience—everyone becomes free in the process. This allows us to consider collective liberation.

Let us begin with an example using the harm that is inflicted upon Black girls in society and how this shows up in schools. In the book *How We Get Free: Black Feminism and the Combahee River Collective*, author Keeanga-Yamahtta Taylor explains the power of centering movements of liberation in, around, and through the lens of womanism. A womanist lens does not in any way suggest that Black women and girls are more important than anyone else, or that we are more important than any other group who may be experiencing oppression. It is necessary, however, to understand the transformation that comes from understanding the unique ways that Black women and girls experience oppression and to use this intersectional understanding to mitigate oppression and move toward healing. To put it more plainly, cisgender Black girls experience oppression because they are Black and because they are girls. This means that Black girls experience sexism and racism simultaneously due to the intersection of these aspects of their identity.

For Black girls who are queer and poor, the oppression they experience is magnified due to poverty, classism, and homophobia. Trans, poor, Black girls whose first language is not English can experience oppression and discrimination due to racism, sexism, transphobia, classism, and educational inequities that are tied to an emphasis on demands around "academic language" and "English-only" spaces in schools. Focusing on the harm that Black girls experience in the world and in schools—and how those harmful practices show up in schools—helps us to work toward healing in a way that is mindful of *all* the ways that our students might experience harm. This intersectional focus allows us to think about, consider, and then act on how Asian American girls may be experiencing harm within our society, how our Black boys are being harmed in society, how our trans students are being harmed within society, and so on. This intersectional approach, when applied to school, helps educators work toward healing no matter where they teach, as they develop an understanding of how and where children are hurting and how this can be healed within learning spaces.

My first suggestion on healing work in schools is for educators to understand how children are harmed. I will continue with my examples of how Black girls are harmed in schools.

Black girls experience oppression based on race and gender identity, as mentioned, and for Black girls who may experience additional forms of oppression, this is magnified. What does this look like in schools?

Black girls in schools are often labeled as defiant, angry, aggressive, and disrespectful. They are often told that they are too loud. They experience adultification, being told, essentially, that their bodies are inappropriate. (Adultification is when girls, especially Black girls, are perceived to be older than they are and receive harsher, developmentally inappropriate punishment or treatment as a result or in response to their behaviors—it might include sexualizing girls' bodies or treating Black girls as though they are adults in matters of discipline.) Black girls who are vocal and opinionated are punished for pushing or "talking back," and when they are silent, they are considered dismissive, defiant, stubborn, or rude. Uniform policies in schools are overwhelmingly used to police girls' bodies. Black girls in schools, too, experience the depths and consequences of toxic masculinity and are sometimes restricted from being able to explore the totality of who they are within a space. Scholar, activist, and filmmaker Monique Couvson (formerly Morris) researches and writes extensively on ways that Black girls are targeted and treated in *Pushout: The Criminalization of Black Girls in Schools* and in *Sing a Rhythm, Dance a Blues: Education for the Liberation of Black and Brown Girls.*

There exists in schools physical harm, emotional harm, mental/psychological harm, and spiritual/soulful harm. In figure 3.1, I am intentional in placing certain actions in multiple places because an action or practice may cause, for example, physical harm, emotional harm, and mental/psychological harm. Then, in figure 3.2, let's look closely at how these manifest for Black girls.

FIGURE 3.1 How Children Are Harmed in Schools

PHYSICAL HARM
- The police or other adults in school who are allowed and given permission to physically harm students' bodies
- The lack of intervention and restoration of student-to-student harm that may exist in schools—the failure to create and sustain spaces in schools that ensure the physical safety of all students
- Calling the police on students
- Overmedicating or sedating students, especially Black students

EMOTIONAL HARM
- Dismissing students' emotions, needs, feelings, and wants
- Prioritizing academics over emotional health and well-being
- Forcing students to suppress what they feel in the name of being "academic" or "right"
- Silencing students
- Creating and sustaining school cultures—reflective of society—that see emotional intelligence or being in tune with emotions as a sign of weakness that has no place in schools
- Embarrassing students
- Shaming students
- Calling the police on students
- Racist hair policies
- Exploiting students for monetary or personal gain

MENTAL/PSYCHOLOGICAL HARM
- School and classroom practices and policies that do not take into account mental health
- Grind culture—no rest, more productivity (overwhelming schedules and amounts of work)

FIGURE 3.1 How Children Are Harmed in Schools, *continued*

- Overmedicating or sedating students, especially Black students
- Dismissing what may be a mental health issue as a behavior problem; responding incorrectly or inappropriately and further exacerbating the issue (one example, rooted in bias, racism, and mental health ignorance, is a Black student being labeled as aggressive, angry, defiant, or disrespectful when, in fact, they may be displaying signs of depression, anxiety, trauma, or other mental health concerns)
- Ignoring, removing, or isolating students with special needs to isolated hallways or basements
- Racist hair policies
- Exploiting students for monetary or personal gain

SPIRITUAL/SOULFUL HARM
- Silencing students' expression by deeming them defiant or disrespectful
- Tone policing, especially Black girls
- Telling Black girls that their facial expressions or gestures are disrespectful, angry, rude, or aggressive
- Not teaching into the ways that students are beautiful, excellent, and worthy
- Demonizing or excluding BIPOC histories and narratives from the curriculum
- Dismissing or shaming students whose spiritual or cultural beliefs may not be considered "mainstream"/white practices
- Forcing students to contort to be deemed successful
- Not allowing forgiveness or for schools and classrooms to be redemptive, restorative spaces

FIGURE 3.2 How Harm Manifests for Black Girls in Schools

TYPE OF HARM	EXAMPLE OF HOW HARM MANIFESTS FOR BLACK GIRLS IN SCHOOLS
Physical	Teachers, administrators, or security/police officers physically harming Black girls. (Videos exist of Black girls being physically harmed in schools, including a particularly disturbing, despicable one of a principal paddling a six-year-old girl of color in Florida.)
Emotional	Black girls being told that they are defiant or disrespectful when expressing themselves. Black girls being told that the tones of their voices, hand gestures, and bodily movements are inappropriate or wrong. Hair policies and practices that suggest Black hair is "wrong," inappropriate, or unprofessional.

continues

FIGURE 3.2 How Harm Manifests for Black Girls in Schools (*continued*)

TYPE OF HARM	EXAMPLE OF HOW HARM MANIFESTS FOR BLACK GIRLS IN SCHOOLS
Mental/ Psychological	An overdiagnosis in schools of Black girls receiving Individualized Education Programs based on "aggressive" behavior. The ignoring and lack of awareness of the ways that mental illness shows up in Black girls. (Often Black girls who may be struggling due to a mental illness may be dismissed as lazy, aggressive, defiant, disrespectful, or disengaged, or as having an attitude problem.)
Spiritual/Soulful	The combination of everything listed in this chart pointing to the spiritual and soulful harm of Black girls: Eurocentric standards of beauty that make Black girls feel as though they are ugly. Sexism, toxic masculinity, and machismo behavior that objectifies Black girls' bodies. The repression of Black girls' sexuality. Internalized racism, such as colorism, which exists in Black and Latinx communities and uniquely harms the spirits of Black and Latina girls. Any behavior that suggests to a Black girl that she is less than or less worthy because of the expressions and existence of her Blackness.

ADDRESS THE HARM WITH HEALING PRACTICES IN THE CLASSROOM

Given the amount and varying types of harm that can and do exist in schools, it is necessary that educators begin to examine how to counteract harmful practices with those that are healing-centered. And so, what does healing look like in schools for Black girls and for other students whose overlapping identities might cause them to experience multiple forms of harm and violence regularly?

Be Intentional About Space

The classroom can be a home for learning. It holds its own unique energy. What students see and feel when they walk into a space signals, often, what the adults who have curated that space think and feel about them.

Space varies based on location, resources, and so on, but physical space, the space where people gather, is incredibly important in healing, belonging, and learning. I have taught in a variety of spaces, and I make a habit of walking through them to get a sense of the energy and to determine how to use the space to create the energy that I think is important for those who will be in it. Preparation for the first day of school provides teachers the opportunity to consider how to welcome students into the learning environment; it sets the tone for the classroom environment. In considering healing spaces, teachers may consider the most inviting seating arrangements, the types of artwork and messaging that should be displayed, and other aesthetics that suggest to students that they are loved, seen, and cared for, that their healing matters, even before they enter the learning space. In my classrooms, I am incredibly intentional about how I decorate the space before students arrive. (I also recognize that schools are resourced differently—some not at all—and decorating may feel like a privilege or a task that is unimportant. Consider how you want students to feel on the first day and how you can authentically communicate that.) I often buy posters and display quotes that are rooted in social justice and love. I include heroes, sheroes, and leaders who look like my students. I also embed a variety of color schemes to make the learning space vibrant and exciting. In some spaces, I bring in live plants or an aromatherapy diffuser so that the space looks and smells good. I usually spent a good amount of time thinking about seating arrangements when I had my own classroom. When possible, I stay away from rigid straight rows, opting for more circular, paired, group, or Socratic seating. Not all schools or spaces allow for this, certainly not during a pandemic, but it is nice to consider when one is able. It is important to me that students feel like it is *their* space.

What does your classroom or learning environment suggest about the space and the students who will inhabit it?

- Do students see themselves reflected in the classroom space?
- What messages, quotes, and inspiration are students able to gather from the space?
- Is the space beautiful, welcoming, and inviting? Is there natural light, does it smell nice? Is the space organized?
- What kinds of expectations do you have for caring for the classroom space?

You should consider not only the physical classroom but the emotional space you provide. Though you do not heal students, you can hold space for students to heal themselves and one another. Do not seek to be your students' saviors, especially white folx. Provide tools and resources for students to explore what may be happening with them. Here are a few ways to start:

- Take pauses and time for students to relax and breathe.
- Create space for students to release. Offer options. When diving into difficult content or topics or when something challenging is happening

in the world, offer time for moments of silence for processing (not necessarily harmful white silence), for students to journal or respond, or to
share thoughts with a partner. Are there opportunities for students to take
a breather, get water, or take a walk when they need some space and time
to process?

- Bring in social workers and counselors when needed.
- Bring in guest writers, poets, or artists to facilitate healing-centered work-
  shops through the arts.
- When something difficult or disastrous happens in the world, hold space.
  Have silent dialogue. (Students may write their thoughts on chart paper or
  sticky notes and express or exchange ideas through writing.) It creates an
  energy in the space where students are not forced to use verbal words or
  expressions. I have done this a number of times, particularly when a Black
  person was killed by the police, and I could *feel* the energy among my
  students. Also, normalize silence when processing hard emotions. Allow
  students to journal through what they may be feeling, to create art if they
  choose. Respect if students do not wish to talk about certain issues with
  you, especially if you are responding to a trauma that may not be a part
  of your lived experience but connects to your students' lived experiences.
  Integrate music within the learning space or allow students to do so if this
  feels good for them.

Preview Content or Texts That May Be Triggering to Students

Healing in our classrooms has direct connections to what it means to be a culturally
responsive practitioner. A part of our work as educators includes teaching texts or
content that may, in fact, be triggering for our students. To center healing in our
learning environments, we must be intentional about how we approach content
or texts that may be triggering to students. As a teacher, it may also be helpful to
familiarize yourself with Stephanie Jones's work on curriculum violence to ensure
that you are not teaching content in ways that are violent to students. Jones defines
curriculum violence as "when educators and curriculum writers have constructed a
set of lessons that damage or otherwise adversely affect students intellectually and
emotionally." When this happens, teachers may be well intentioned, but the impact
is damaging. Jones uses an example of one of her first teachers making students pick
cotton so that they would understand how difficult it is. Other examples include having students learn about slavery by "*practicing* being enslaved people or enslavers."[3]

There are some things to consider and actions you might take when you preview content for triggers:

- Explain to students what you will be teaching in the upcoming unit or lesson and why they are learning about this. Allow students to share their thoughts, feelings, questions, or challenges with the material. This can be through an in-class discussion or in written form. You could also make yourself available for one-on-one conversations during student conferencing or office hours.
- If you are choosing media material, such as videos, music, films, or documentaries, consider how students might feel watching this and determine whether it is necessary to show in your classroom. Again, inform yourself about curriculum violence to ensure you are not doing this, and if you are not sure, always ask others. As educators, we must do our due diligence, research, read as much as we can, and speak to other educators and community members.
- Allow other forms of viewing, such as watching at home or offering supplementary content.
- Decide if there are other ways to teach the content using material that will not be triggering.
- Allow plenty of space and room for students to process (to reflect, to discuss, to be silent, and to move their bodies as needed).
- When appropriate, write home to families, parents, and caregivers so that they have a sense of the material that may be taught in class, and invite their input. Too often in schools of largely Black and Latinx students, there exists a complete dismissal of the voices of parents or caregivers in the education of their own children.
- Call on community members, professionals, organizations, and social work or counseling teams when needed.

I called on other professionals when I taught Maya Angelou's *I Know Why the Caged Bird Sings*. I had previewed the content of this memoir well before students began reading; I knew Angelou had been raped at a young age, and that students would read about it in the book. To prepare students, I invited our school social worker into the classroom to lead conversations on sexual assault and rape. What allowed me to teach this text, more than anything else, was the foundation I had built all year. I was confident in my strong relationships with my students. I knew they felt comfortable sharing their thoughts and experiences with me—through writing, class conversations, and one-on-one. Otherwise, I would not have engaged in this particular text or pushed against administration on how to best teach it.

Because I employed a number of healing practices in the classroom and because writing and discussions, specifically, can both open up wounds and create mechanisms for healing, students often wrote in their journals and confided in me about their personal lives and experiences. Students understood that I was a mandated reporter and what that meant. Additionally, I worked closely with our social work and counseling teams because of the sheer amount of information that students shared in our space. I was not, am not, a trained psychologist or mental health professional. I wanted to do my best to support students and to honor their vulnerability, but I encouraged them to see our social workers and counselors and to seek outside help when needed.

Healing Through Writing

There are a number of ways to include healing forms of writing within the classroom. This includes:

- brief and daily journaling
- allowing students to make personal connections to the content
- allowing students to share their writing with each other or aloud when they feel compelled (I learned, as I grew in my teaching career, the importance of allowing students to offer their work and of sharing rather than forcing everyone to do so. I am so grateful for the ways I have had to learn and correct by hearing my students)
- allowing students to demonstrate their learning and feelings through poetry or song (again, this can be done across disciplines)
- allowing students to write about what challenges them, what they enjoy, and what questions they have in regard to the material.

Honor Culturally Responsive Ways of Healing

Forms of healing vary based on culture. One way that racism, specifically, blocks healing is by dismissing or demonizing forms of healing that are not rooted in white, Eurocentric, or Western ways of healing. This is a form of harm rooted deeply in colonization, enslavement, and racism. For many cultures within the African diaspora, dancing, storytelling, connecting to a higher power, connecting to and honoring ancestors and spirit, laughing, crying, and shouting are ways of healing, releasing, and being present with and moving through pain. There are many ways to honor various and cultural forms of healing:

- Ask students to discuss and share what healing looks like in their homes or culture.
- Allow students to regularly interact with, learn from, and demonstrate learning and feeling through music and through the arts.
- Teach explicitly into and about healing, and dismiss this notion that Western ways of healing, religion, or medicine are *right*. This is something students should be able to determine for themselves. Read stories, as well as experiencing videos, films, and other media that explore the multitude of ways that people heal.
- For Black students, teach and name the ways that healing looks both differently and similarly throughout the African diaspora.
- Restore and honor the arts. One of the biggest forms of the impact of racism in schools and assaults on Black healing, specifically, is the removal of the arts in schools. Many cultures and bodies of color are deeply rooted in and tied to the performing arts. Storytelling, visual arts, music, dance, and creating with our hands are an integral part of the Black experience, our experience, and our healing. Restoring and centering the arts has looked like this in my classroom:
  - Allow students to write creatively every day.
  - Provide varying forms of assessments—I call these demonstrations of learning—that include the performing arts. Allow students to show what they know through creating dances, skits, plays, and songs.
  - Teach about various aspects of history and culture through the arts and through food. (Teachers seeking this approach should do so critically and mindfully. Having students bring in dishes that represent entire cultures could be problematic. It could also be considered curriculum violence. One way to honor cultures, history, and healing through food might be similar to what I did a number of times with soul food. I designed lessons around Black history, reclamation, enslavement,

resistance, and joy and then encouraged students to make connections to various forms of soul food. In addition to eating, students engaged in research and discussions.) This is also a form of joy!

· Take students on field trips to arts-centered places.
· Normalize the arts and create a learning space in which the arts are as valuable as other forms of learning and assessment.
· Allow students to use art to think through and process challenging emotions, thoughts, or content.

PLEASE NOTE:
TAKE TIME TO BECOME A CULTURALLY RESPONSIVE TEACHER

For some of my teaching suggestions, please note the amount of time, energy, and practice that I have intentionally placed into being a culturally responsive and critical educator. These practices are not meant to be merely replicated. Take the time and due diligence to build yourself as a critical, culturally responsive educator and think deeply before implementing.

Center and Allow for Movement
in the Classroom (When It Can Be Done Safely)

▪ Acknowledge the body *and* the brain in teaching.
▪ Allow movement breaks. Please also consider ability justice and what movement may or may not look like for disabled students.
▪ Allow students to express themselves through dance. There are connections that can be explored, examined, and explained through dance, including those to science (energy, matter, biology, health), math (rhythm, counting, steps, beats), and the humanities (storytelling and analysis).
▪ Allow students to move throughout the course of learning with stations teaching, working in groups or partners, working on the floor if they wish, and spreading out and working.

Allow Multiple Demonstrations of Learning as a Way of Honoring
Cultural Practices and Ways of Expressing Knowledge

Tests and summative assessments should not be the only acceptable way for students to demonstrate knowledge and learning, especially for students belonging to cultures where oral expression, movement, and art are a part of how they have historically expressed themselves. Figure 3.3 shows other ways students can demonstrate learning.

FIGURE 3.3 Multiple Demonstrations of Learning in My Classroom

Oral tradition (speeches, storytelling, reciting poetry, spoken word, rap, and song)	One beautiful practice that I implemented in my classroom was guiding students through creating their own narratives/memoirs. In some of the schools where I taught, students put on poetry café events to showcase their work to the community. Another year, students published their memoirs and poetry anthologies! Each year during the month of April, students engaged in a poetry unit. We read poems by a number of authors, especially authors of color. Each unit culminated with students creating original poems. Figure 3.4 shows an excerpt of an anthology that tenth-grader Anaiyah put together for our poetry unit. In teaching Shakespearean texts—something students may not have been thrilled about—students explained what was happening or what they understand about the text through their own songs. Students also put on plays and skits. To teach literary analysis or literary devices, I used music, especially rap, for students to analyze rhetorical and literacy devices and theme. For example, students analyzed Tupac's or Kendrick Lamar's use of imagery and metaphor to communicate a critical theme around a social injustice. (I will also note that this is something I did regularly in my classroom, so inserting a rap song for a lesson did not feel performative. Teachers should be mindful of this.)
Art (painting, sculpture, and comics)	For an "Art as Resistance" event, some of my tenth-grade students created sculptures, paintings, and other forms of visual art to communicate information about and to resist social injustices within the Dominican Republic. Often, students were given the option to create graphic novels or comic strips to demonstrate their analysis of a text.
Multimedia (documentary and public service announcement)	For a communications unit, my tenth-grade students created original documentaries on social injustices, such as domestic violence, poverty, and bullying, that they were passionate about combatting within their communities. Students created and shared public service announcements on social injustices for a rhetoric unit.
Movement (dance)	During the study of *Romeo and Juliet*, students researched the Elizabethan era. I co-choreographed a dance within the style of the era for students to engage in with one another. I have also created demonstrations of learning to show how students could use dance to communicate themes or ideas we explored within a text.
Performance (theatre, skits, and tableaux)	Students almost always engaged in performance as part of a major assessment, including: • poetry cafés at the end of a poetry unit • putting on plays after studying the work of a major playwright • creating a tableau or skit to reveal themes within a text • putting on an "Art as Resistance" event tackling social injustices through multiple art forms • performing an original dance piece interpreting the emotions a student experiences when reading a poem

FIGURE 3.4 Excerpts from *Anaiyah's Poetry Anthology*

Dear Reader,

Welcome to my life. In this anthology, you will learn so much about me. Like where I am from, what I like to do, who I am, what I believe in, and what I have experienced. I wrote a majority of this anthology in my English class during a poetry unit. I really pushed myself to write about topics I find emotionally draining such as the loss of my grandparents. My grandparents were my world, and they still are. They supported anything I did because they always thought I had the potential to do great things. They taught me to be a fearless woman filled with patience and love. They encouraged me to be the best version of myself every single day I have on this Earth. One day, I told my grandparents I wanted to be an author. They brought me so many notebooks and pens and told me to write about everything that has ever made me curious or anything that has impacted me. Since I was young at the time and I did not know what the word "impacted" meant, I did not understand how valuable this piece of advice was. But now that I'm older and I know what "impacted" means, I have been using their advice since. I believe firmly, you can never write a decent piece about something you are not passionate about or affected by—no matter what the subject matter is. Writing is all storytelling and perspective. When we write, we are enabling readers to see what we see. Always remember to tell *your* story.

—Anaiyah

I Remember

I remember my childhood
I knew exactly what I wanted to be
I was determined to become a crossing guard
I thought making all the hand gestures to direct cars would be fun
And that I would have so much fun blowing the whistle, and walking the elderly
    and children down the street
I remember my childhood

My mother tucked me into bed and my dad would read me books
Before I dreamt of living in a pink castle
I was convinced Justin Bieber and I would get married
And we would have a dog together named Terry
I had no worries
I had no doubt

FIGURE 3.4 Excerpts from *Anaiyah's Poetry Anthology, continued*

I wish I could turn back to those times

When innocence and happiness radiated off my skin

When I did not know what death was, what pain felt like, what problems were

Because when we were children, all the evil was tucked away with the monsters
*   we thought were under our beds*

All the evil was hidden under pillows with our teeth

Concealed in layers of wrapping paper placed on toys

Tucked in the bushes with chocolate eggs

Frozen with the ice cream on the back of the truck

Dangling from trees while we were on the monkey bars

We were vulnerable kids

Lured into all the evil this world has to offer

out of the blue, the evil unveiled itself

I have not been the same since

Nobody has

I remember my childhood vividly

In This One You Are

In this one you are laughing uncontrollably

In your living room

Holding the dolls I made you grasp

I did your makeup and handed you the mirror

I thought the makeup looked great

But you looked like a circus clown

You were wearing the hat I made you out of newspaper and tape

Sitting on the couch

Full of life and spirit

Thinking about it now, I still hear your harmonic voice

Telling me to snap another photo while you did a ridiculous pose

And I can smell your heavy perfume and your warm cookies in the oven

That day, you made me feel full of life and spirit

And now that you're gone, I don't think I can ever feel that way again

All I have is this picture of us

With bent corners and fading colors

continues

FIGURE 3.4 Excerpts from *Anaiyah's Poetry Anthology, continued*

You are the reason

You are the reason I wake up everyday
And cry,
The reason my walls are built so high,
The reason I do not think I deserve happiness.
You, are the reason I lost direction
I lost myself, you're the reason why.

QUESTIONS FOR TEACHERS TO CONSIDER

1. What are your thoughts on the role of healing after reading this chapter?
2. What is the role of healing in liberatory teaching?
3. What might a healing-centered classroom or school look like for you?
4. What challenges are you anticipating?
5. What research or sources will you dive further into after reading this chapter?
6. What are some tools or strategies that you'd like to implement right away?
7. What will you need in order to center healing in your work?

CHAPTER 4

HEALING AND SELF-CARE FOR TEACHERS

Self-care is not selfish. You cannot
be an effective educator if you are not well.

—JAMILAH PITTS

As a teacher, I struggled to find balance between my work and life, and it cost me in ways that I am still healing from. I experienced increasing amounts of guilt and truly believed that to provide my students with what they needed, I had to work constantly. It is important for educators to understand that to center liberation, to center the well-being and overall success of our students, we have to also protect our health and well-being. Moreover, it is also important to know how the disregard for teacher burnout and deep disregard for wellness and healing are also tools of oppression.

MY HEALING JOURNEY

After taking some time to process the harm, trauma, and abuse that led me to resign from working as a school leader, I decided to write about my experiences and the need to protect Black women in schools in a *Learning for Justice* article in 2021:

> I have been asked for quite some time to chronicle why I left working in schools directly, and why I made the decision to resign from my position as school leader . . . midyear. The hard truth is that this has taken so long to write because I have been on my own healing journey, sitting deep in self-reflection and working to heal the harm, trauma, and PTSD that I regularly experience from my time working in schools. It has been a long journey, a beautiful one at times, but also a visceral

one, as friends, family, coaches, and mentors helped me to see the ways in which working and leading in schools stripped me of so much of my power that it has taken, even still, years to reclaim and to fully heal.[1]

I wrote this piece not as a lament over my experiences as a Black woman working in a leadership position in schools serving predominantly Black and Latinx children, but rather to lay bare and give voice to many of the harmful practices that exist in schools, many of which are deeply rooted in systemic racism, internalized oppression, patriarchy, and capitalism that collectively work together to create a brutal environment for Black women's bodies and psyches. I hope that school and system leaders will use this as a guide to understand how to create equitable and sustainable spaces for Black women who are in many ways both the backbones of society and of schools where large populations of Black students are served.

Racism destroys Black women because the construction of race, patriarchy, and sexism work in tandem to reinforce and create harmful predicaments and conditions that lead to and sustain gender discrimination. Capitalism creates and sustains painful living experiences for those most impacted by poverty; and in schools, the focus on monetary gain creates working conditions that are particularly crushing for Black bodies. The legendary Zora Neale Hurston captures this sentiment in *Their Eyes Were Watching God*, explaining that Black women are "the mules of the world."[2]

WAYS IN WHICH BLACK WOMEN ARE UNIQUELY HARMED

As educators and leaders seek to create equitable school spaces, including equity for staff and students, it is imperative that we consider the ways that Black women are uniquely harmed. To do so, we must be vigilant in understanding that schools are microcosms of society, that schools mirror the systems of inequity and harmful practices that exist outside of school doors. It must be understood that if the adults who are serving our young people are not well, then young people cannot be served well. Here are some of the ways that schooling systems were destructive for me as a leader and point to ways that they might also be harmful for other Black women.

The "Angry Black Woman"

Over the course of my career, I have been called various iterations of an "angry Black woman" by both white people and Black men. Some used the direct term, while others used passive-aggressive language, such as "non-jovial" to describe my being and stance. This term, this labeling, this aggression toward Black women also exists in schools. Because schools are institutions that are rooted in white supremacy culture and are positioned to uphold white and Eurocentric ideas of success, this, too, comes crashing down on Black women in ways that are destructive. Black women in society and in schools are often judged by measures of whiteness, and when it comes to how we express our views, our emotions, our body language, and our facial expressions, Black women are often measured by ideas that are rooted in white women's ways of being and how they express themselves. Black women who do not possess a proximity to whiteness are deemed angry when we voice our opinions, set boundaries, or disagree publicly, or we are labeled so for simply being. For not smiling or laughing enough, for being firm or having high expectations, for demanding respect. Our very tones, the way we sound, how we express emotion are often deemed inappropriate, rude, angry, or disrespectful because we exist within a society that has long demanded our silence, production of children, or submission. Anything outside of that is deemed unacceptable. And sometimes, painfully, this violence comes directly from other Black women.

The "Strong, Superhuman" Black Woman

The myth of the strong or superhuman Black woman is also rampant and harmful in schools. As I noted in the article for *Learning for Justice*, "Black women are expected to endure all things, to be all things and to be excellent at all things, especially as it relates to Black children. While Black women are gifted, powerful and beautiful; we are also human. Failure to see the humanity of Black women in schools often leads to overburdening Black women with responsibilities, expecting Black women always to be 'on' and hold space for others."[3] (There is an unspoken expectation in schools that Black women, in our nuance and giftedness, can do everything, that we can never be weak or ill, and that we lack humanity. This comes crashing down so deeply on Black women who are already unseen.)

Respectability Politics

The politics of respectability—the idea that Black people are only worthy of respect when we meet certain criteria (we are educated, have lighter skin, are meek and quiet, are "qualified," "speak well/are articulate," are "successful")—has long existed within Black history and culture in America. Some may argue that it has been inextricably linked to Black people's ability to survive, and others recognize its harmful impact because (1) Black people are not a monolith, and (2) there is the recognition that politics of respectability are rooted in ideas of what is "successful" and, therefore, worthy of respect according to white standards of being. In schools, this is particularly harmful for Black staff members, especially Black women. This manifests in a number of ways but includes pathways to leadership for Black women being wrapped up in and measured by a Black woman's proximity to whiteness. Many Black women educators will admit or share that to achieve, attain promotions, or become leaders—despite their expertise and knowledge of Black children—they had to contort, shrink, and become less of themselves to be respected. This looks like agreeing with policies that are harmful so that they are not labeled as difficult; choosing not to speak up in meetings on behalf of children or about harm they have experienced or witnessed; pretending to be OK with toxic leadership, practices, and policies to advance; or agreeing to demonize or harm other Black staff in the name of aligning themselves so that they can move ahead.

Internalized Racism and Sexism

While working in schools, I experienced a range of harmful interactions from both BIPOC staff, particularly Black staff and leaders, and white leaders. Sadly, harmful interactions from white staff are unsurprising, but it is also worth mentioning the ways that Black people uniquely internalize our oppression, and when we are unaware of this harm, we tend to harm those who look like us. This causes deep psychological pain because the toxic behaviors are, essentially, coming from people who look like you. Much of the negative feedback I received from other school leaders in the school I resigned from were, in fact, from other Black women or toxic Black men. Although many schools are working to examine the ways that they uphold or perpetuate racist ideas and practices, schools must also be vigilant in considering the ways that Black people come to believe, internalize, and regurgitate the ideas, practices, beliefs, and philosophies that surround us in a culture that praises and centers white ways of being. Many Black people, to make it into positions of school leadership, have to play upon double and, for Black women, triple consciousness. We have to navigate within, outside, around, and through the various forms of oppression that seek to harm us. Internalized racism and sexism in schools looks and sounds like this:

- Black women who grow up in a culture that deeply devalues us being unable to see the power and beauty within themselves and therefore being unable to see the power and beauty in other Black women
- Black women competing with other Black women because of a belief that only so many of "us" can "make it"

- Women body-shaming other women and girls
- Black women being silent or complicit in the harm against other Black women as a means to protect themselves, their path, and their upward mobility
- Black women labeling other Black women as difficult or angry
- Black women tone-policing other Black women
- Black women refusing to speak up for other Black women who are experiencing harm because they want to "get ahead"
- Black women criticizing the facial and bodily expressions of other Black women (women telling other women to "fix their face")

It is also important to name that internalized oppression and internalized racism are forms of racism and to point to additional ways that racism can manifest in schools. This is why healing is so important among Black staff members who are working together in schools. Without conversations on what is truly happening and driving our behavior, we tend to perpetuate cycles of harm against each other.

WAYS IN WHICH SCHOOLS ARE HARMFUL TO THE ADULTS WHO SERVE OUR YOUNG PEOPLE

In schools where the student body is predominantly Black and Brown, there exists a deep and toxic burnout culture tied to both racism and capitalism. There is a resounding belief that to "save" children (which is also deeply problematic and racist) everyone must work harder and longer. In my experience and observation, this rings particularly true for Black staff in predominantly Black schools because we innately understand that our success, our ability to thrive, is connected to the children who look like us. Although this connection and understanding is not inherently bad, the ways that we tend to overextend ourselves to correct wrongs and ills we did not create are, in fact, harmful to our well-being.

Toxic Burnout Culture

In schools, toxic burnout culture is tied to both racism and capitalism. Capitalism demands that staff work hard to repair systems of inequity to ensure that students learn so that they can become members of society who produce deeper monetary gain for our country. It is tied in many ways to labor and production. Toxic burnout culture is tied to racism because racism and capitalism have long reinforced each other in this country.

Toxic burnout culture in schools also manifests in other ways. Extended school days and extended school years are used to reinforce the belief that if children and adults work harder, the children will perform better. Measurements of academic performance, however, are often racist (e.g., standardized exams) and tied to monetary gain. There is also the belief that if teachers work harder, disparities will disappear. This is a false narrative because the disparities exist due to factors such as systemic racism, poverty, and capitalism.

The Harmful Praise for a Deep Lack of Self-Care

When I work in schools, I often seek to set boundaries to preserve my physical, mental, and emotional health. In doing so, I've been told by leaders that I was "selfish," that my "wellness had to look different because I was a leader," that I was not "a team player." Failure to allow teachers to be human also looks like this:

- demonizing teachers who call out of work to care for themselves
- dismissing the need for mental health days for staff
- telling staff that they are selfish or are not team players for setting boundaries or saying no
- maintaining expectations that teachers always arrive early and stay late
- creating a staff culture that rewards overworking and demonizing staff who refuse to do so. (I understand why teachers work so hard, especially in schools serving BIPOC students, but burning teachers out is never the answer.)

SELF-CARE AND WELLNESS PRACTICES FOR TEACHERS

Racism, sexism, transphobia, homophobia, and an overreliance on harmful traits of capitalism rob each of us of our collective humanity. I do not believe that those who are fully bought into ideas of harming others, ideas of domination, are fully in touch with their humanity. It simply is not possible to fully love yourself and seek to harm others. Self-care and wellness are integral to effective teaching, and they are integral to working toward collective liberation. If we do not first fully love ourselves, if we are not fully well, whole, and rested, we *cannot* and we *are not* fully able to work toward the collective healing and liberation of others. To be fully present with the self, to be fully mindful, to be fully connected to the aspects of our being undoubtedly and subsequently awakens us to the suffering of others.

I am sure we are all familiar with the old adage "you cannot pour from an empty cup." This is true, and it has to be true if we are educators, and particularly if we are educators seeking to center liberation within and throughout our practices. Teaching, in general, can feel like a sacrifice. As educators we spend the year—despite having breaks throughout the summer and over holidays—thinking about our students, preparing for them, and thinking about ways to deepen and expand our practice. Teaching is heart work, and it demands so much of us, mentally, physically, emotionally, and spiritually. Teaching for liberation asks that we tap into our innermost being. To be an effective educator, and certainly an educator who centers liberation, we *have* to be well.

One of the most damaging comments I heard in my career as an educator, particularly as a leader, was that "my wellness had to look differently as a leader" and that I "got paid" to work extensively longer than what my contract actually dictated. It has taken me a while to do so, but I extend grace and a level of understanding to those who made the comments and for those of us who may feel that there is truth and validity in the statements. As liberatory educators, we have to be willing to grapple with "truths" that are harmful and adopt a willingness to embrace practices rooted in liberation, wholeness, and love.

I have long held the mantra of scholar-warrior and poet Audre Lorde: "Caring for myself is not self-indulgence, it is self-preservation, and that is an act of political warfare."[4]

For those of us, especially Black women, who inhabit bodies of culture and color, as healer and therapist Resmaa Menakem explains it, our ability to choose ourselves, our wellness, our joy, and our rest is an act of political warfare; it is protest; it is resistance. American history and society have long demanded labor and production—in the name of advancing and perpetuating capitalism and exploitation—from Black bodies, especially Black women's bodies. To truly understand how wellness and self-care are forms of resistance, particularly within the field of education, we have to examine the harmful impacts of capitalism paired with racism and patriarchy. These collective systems of oppression—or domination—demand more, vilify rest, and praise work because it is tied to economic gain. Although economic gain is not entirely harmful (especially for people who have been historically marginalized and disenfranchised), the consistent practice and building of systems around wealth, labor, and economic gain at the risk of killing people is harmful. This happens all too much in Western cultures, particularly within education.

Because the teaching profession is largely female, I believe that there is a great disdain for rest and an utter disrespect for what women need to be well. History points to this. Particularly for Black women who are teaching Black children, there is an expectation that we be the doers and holders of all things. We are conditioned and taught that generosity, particularly sacrifice, is a virtue when it comes to our children—be it those who we birth from our bodies or those who are placed under our care as educators. Additionally, for Black women educators, at least in my experience, these beliefs are deep-seated when we are serving children who look like us because we know and understand that the freedom, health, and wealth of our children are inextricably linked to our own ability to experience full liberation. We have a deep understanding of the importance of the collective and truly see our children. This can show up in our practices in ways that can be beneficial to our overall well-being. To be healthy, we have to be willing to divorce ideas of self-care from selfishness.

As a daughter of a single parent, I know that self-care is something that feels generationally new for many Black women. We can demonize ourselves and even one another for choosing self, rest, and our wellness—particularly over the needs of children—because this simply has not been modeled for us.

Where and How Do We Begin to Care for Ourselves?

We have to be willing to embrace a new pathway forward. It is OK to know and act on the truth that we cannot do for others if we have not first taken care of ourselves, and we cannot give what we do not have. This is true for all educators, but particularly true for Black women educators serving Black children. We are not lesser educators or lesser leaders because we set boundaries, use "No" as a complete sentence, or refuse to explain our reasonings for taking time off or for prioritizing our well-being. I encourage educators to use your paid time off. We are better educators when we are able to care first for ourselves. So, how do we do this in ways that honor our healing?

1. We recognize and shift our mindsets around self-care and wellness. We embrace new beliefs around the importance of prioritizing our well-being and healing so that we are able to then give to our students.
2. We recognize that, as educators, we are our best when we serve and create from a place of wholeness and rest rather than a place of need or guilt or because we feel unworthy and are using work and outputs to prove our worthiness. We affirm for ourselves that *we are worthy; therefore, we are worthy of rest, of self-care, and of pleasure.*

3. We take the time to get to know ourselves and what we need, and we seek to first meet those needs. I like to use a wheel of self-care to help me with this (see figure 4.1).

4. We encourage and affirm one another in our practices to ensure that we are well, and we have crucial conversations with those who seek to demonize those who know that self-care is not selfish.

5. We build sustainable practices around our self-care and wellness that make sense for our lives and resources (see figure 4.2).

6. We encourage and model for our students what it means to care for ourselves.

7. We create communities of self-care, self-love, and belonging that lend themselves to social justice, healing, joy, and liberation for all, particularly those who are marginalized (e.g., affinity spaces for BIPOC staff, self-care and wellness committees, accountability partners and groups, connections with wellness professionals and healers rooted in social justice, healing, and trauma-informed practices in our lives and work).

Use This Self-Care Wheel to Create and Deepen Your Self-Care Practice

FIGURE 4.1 Self-Care Wheel

- Your physical health
  - What do you need to be physically well?
  - How is your body and overall physical health?
  - Do you have measures in place for your annual health check-ins?

- Your mental health
  - What do you need to be mentally well?
  - How would you describe your mental health?
  - Are you open to seeking mental health support if you feel that you need it? Why or why not?
  - What support do you have in place to ensure that you are mentally well?

- Your emotional health
  - How is your emotional self? How would you describe it?
  - What do you need to ensure that you are emotionally well?

- Your spiritual health
  - If this applies and you have a spiritual practice:
    - How is your overall spiritual life?
    - What do you need to be well spiritually?

- Your personal goals
  - What personal goals do you have for yourself?
  - How are you making time to protect and pursue your personal goals?

- Your financial goals
  - How is your financial life or your relationship with finances?
  - If money feels like a hindrance or source of stress for you, are you able to identify why? What do you need to be financially well?
  - What financial goals do you have for yourself?
  - Do you have or might you consider joining a group or finding a financial advisor to support you with your financial goals and planning?

- Your professional goals
  - What are your dreams, goals, and aspirations?

Take Steps to Build a Teacher Routine Rooted in Self-Care and Love

FIGURE 4.2 Teacher Routine Steps

1. Your morning routine:
   - What is a good time for you to rise so that you have time for a routine that allows you to pour into self before others?
   - Are you able to allow for some sort of physical activity in the morning, even if it is only a few minutes (stretching, yoga, a run or walk), that works for your abilities within your body?
   - What nourishing foods can you put into your body in the morning to get you started?
   - Mind things: do you have access to affirmations, a reading, a podcast, a song that refreshes you in the morning and sets you up for success?
   - Set an intention: take some time to say and lay out an intention for your day.
   - Complete these things for you and then focus on others and on work.

   My morning routine often looked like this when teaching:

   Woke up at 5:15 a.m.

   Took a quick stretch in bed.

   Shower + affirmation + spiritual practice. I combined my affirmations, intentions, and spiritual practice with something I did every morning (e.g., showering) so that I did not skip it. I prayed, meditated, or set an intention while showering. My written affirmations were on my bathroom mirror so I saw them as I was getting ready.

   I grabbed my water, tea, smoothie, and lunch (if I had prepped the meal), and while getting my bags ready for the day, I listened to soft music, yoga music, a favorite playlist, or worship music. Now I light incense and drink lemon water while doing this.

   I took a few minutes (usually no more than five) for a quick yoga practice, or on some days a few breaths in child's pose, and then I was out of the door by 6:30 a.m.

   When I arrived to work—early so that I could get more time for prep and mental preparation before others arrived—I had my breakfast, a cup of tea (usually aligned with what I needed: a green tea if I needed energy or a calming tea if I felt anxious about the day), and then I began to check and respond to emails or engage in other tasks.

continues

FIGURE 4.2 Teacher Routine Steps, *continued*

2. Your plan for nourishing meals:

Food is so important for our work. I learned in my first year of teaching that I could not eat foods that drained my energy, or I would feel heavy or irritable, and I simply could not be my best self for my students. Many educators prep meals because time can be so difficult to come by, or we resort to eating foods that are not life-giving. In my case, when working in schools in New York City, I developed a number of mental health and physical issues because I did not always have the time to go out to grab lunch or did not have the energy to prep meals.

So, what is your plan for nourishing meals? Some ideas might include:

- prepping your meal ahead of time
- choosing a special day of the week to order food in (I know it felt difficult to leave the building to get food at times.)
- pairing up with teacher friends (e.g., potlucks so that you prep and have multiple options for food for the week; take turns grabbing meals for one another)
- forming food committees so that teams can take turns bringing food for staff
- using a cookbook or blog
- looking into, or consulting your doctor or a healer, on the best types of food for your body (I used a combination of working with energy healers and diving into Ayurveda and herbalism to develop the best diet for me, a mostly plant-based or highly anti-inflammatory diet.)
- creating a plan for meals that work for and nourish you!

3. Make time for your joy, pleasure, and fun. For me, this looks like:

- having time with friends
- planning vacations that coincided with school breaks to places I always wanted to visit (Mentally, this also got me through hard stretches in the year.)
- going to brunch on the weekends
- going to yoga
- investing in my dating life
- dancing
- working with a financial advisor to set financial goals
- saving up to get massages or facials
- investing in little steps that would allow me to one day start my own business
- treating myself . . . often!

4. Build a wellness community for yourself of people who love you and will encourage you to be well!

QUESTIONS FOR TEACHERS TO CONSIDER

1. Where are you in your beliefs and mindset regarding *your* self-care?
2. What obstacles or hindrances exist around a self-care practice for yourself? Are there any?
3. Are there any suggestions from this chapter that you can implement right away?
4. What does healing mean and look like for you?

CHAPTER 5

TEACHING AS LOVE

When I began writing this book, we were not where we are now as a nation. Breonna Taylor was still alive, George Floyd had not yet been brutally murdered by a police officer, and we had not yet entered the season of a (long overdue) racial awakening and a deeper return to human consciousness. There did not yet exist political and social wars around anti-racist practices, "The 1619 Project," and critical race theory. Yet, as I write this chapter and complete this book, here we are.

For those of us who have the privilege of leading and working alongside young people (truly they lead us), we ought to embrace the idea that the pursuit of liberation—at the end of the day—is about love. It is radical love.

Anti-racist educators believe in love. Many educators operate from the premise that they love their students. In fact, many harmful and violent teachers operate from a place of "love." But anti-racist educators understand that love and silence are deeply contradictory. The love that underpins our practice is not the form of love often associated with passivity and inaction. For anti-racist educators, love is action. Love is sharp. Love is truthtelling. Love is fighting for what it is right. Love is *doing* what is right.

Anti-racist educators, particularly those who teach Black students, understand that part of the act of love is understanding what this country has *intentionally* done—and continues to do—to Black bodies. It is love that compels our practices.

Anti-racist educators understand that, in love, they must never be silent. *Ever.* Anti-racist educators understand that their positions as teachers, leaders, policymakers, and social workers are positions of great privilege and power, and that they have the ability to leave this world better than they found it.[1]

Educators are among the most loving people on this planet. That love compels us, guides us to, and sustains us in our practices as educators. To work toward and sustain liberation within and through our field, we have to sit down with, crack open, and examine what it means to love.

DEVELOP A LOVE ETHOS

Love—like teaching—can benefit from some redefining and radicalizing. The two are often conflated with "feel goodness" (which is not inherently a bad thing), passivity, docility, and inaction. Like love, teaching can be in some ways romanticized. Because educators work with children and young people, there is often a notion that our work must always be sweet and gentle, that our role is to tend to the children and ensure they are loved and well, and that children must be in some way shielded from the realities of the world. Our definition of love in mainstream society, too, is often reduced to romance, butterflies—one aspect of love—and not on the relationship, the work, and the action that surrounds it.

The work and scholarship of bell hooks around love as a freedom practice is deeply useful in the pursuit of liberation in an educational space. She writes:

> Without love, our efforts to liberate ourselves and our world community from oppression and exploitation are doomed. As long as we refuse to address fully the place of love in struggles for liberation, we will not be able to create a culture of conversion where there is a mass turning away from an ethic of domination.[2]

Although much of my work in this chapter is rooted in combating racism in educational settings with predominantly Black students, I urge each of us to adopt and put into practice an intersectional approach to justice, freedom, and healing. I share often in my work with schools that "anti" practices fail to be effective if we are not considering all forms of oppression. In liberation practices, which cannot be achieved without the presence of love, we must consider not only racism, but patriarchy, capitalism, homophobia, transphobia, xenophobia, and all other forms of prejudice, injustice, and oppression. Love both drives us to liberatory practices and pursuits—true love for self, which allows us to love others—and allows us to sustain liberatory pursuits and practices. And to *truly* love means that we are seeking to end all forms of domination.

Liberation, or any form of transformation, cannot be achieved without love, compassion, and empathy. As bell hooks reminds us, "A culture of domination is anti-love."[3] The Western world, particularly within the United States—deeply rooted in capitalism, production, and competition—praises and ultimately devalues love, particularly love in action. In the workforce, a love ethic is frowned upon, discouraged, deemed inappropriate. Love is viewed as a weakness, unless it can be monetized. Fortunately, for teachers and educators, love underpins our work. *Or at least it ought to.* We use the term often and recognize that teaching is both "heart" work and hard work and that to truly be effective we must love not only our craft but our children.

When teachers recognize our power—and I know it is hard to do so within a system that devalues the field of K–12 teaching—we are able to understand that our profession has a direct impact on what people will come to know, believe, and do. If teachers do not act on and from a place of love, we continue to reinforce and perpetuate forms of oppression that will never move our society forward.

This feels like a tall task for educators, especially when they have increasingly full loads, but there are ways to reexamine and approach our crafts differently in ways that reinforce love. I trust that most educators are beautiful, well-intentioned people. I trust that educators love their students, but a part of acting on that love means working for and toward liberation, mitigating harm, and teaching our students in ways that allow them to foster deep love for self and for others. Figure 5.1 shows what love in teaching looks like and what it does not look like.

FIGURE 5.1 Love in Teaching

LOVE IN TEACHING LOOKS LIKE	LOVE IN TEACHING DOES NOT LOOK LIKE
• Teaching the *whole* child; seeing the child as a human being who has varying needs and understanding that to teach the whole child means understanding all aspects of who that child is • Learning about students' cultures, backgrounds, and experiences • Seeing caregivers and parents as experts on their own children • Creating classroom environments that cherish student voices • Empathizing with people, including young people • Doing your due diligence in understanding your students' experiences, histories, backgrounds, and cultures • Centering critical thinking	• Centering Eurocentric or white ideas, practices, and beliefs • Exploiting children, especially poor children of color • Believing that it is OK for teachers to take a place of neutrality in a world and within a profession where oppression exists and is perpetuated • Asserting force, domination, and privilege over students (taking a stance that suggests that teachers know all things and are the only powerful individuals within a learning space) • Employing whitewashed curriculum, curriculum that is violent, curriculum that does not center stories and experiences of people of the Global Majority, or curriculum that reinforces styles of learning rooted in whiteness

continues

FIGURE 5.1 Love in Teaching, *continued*

LOVE IN TEACHING LOOKS LIKE	LOVE IN TEACHING DOES NOT LOOK LIKE
• Creating a classroom environment that is reflective of who students are • Creating a classroom environment and embracing a teaching and learning practice that honor the multiple ways students learn • Apologizing when we harm students • Taking care of ourselves so that we are showing up and teaching students from a place of fullness, rather than a place of need, lack, frustration, or despair • Humility • Constant learning • Cultivating joy • Being anti-racist, antibias, and anti-oppression; being against all forms of discrimination and domination	• Emphasizing standardized testing and grind culture • Penalizing Black students for being human • Silencing students • Demanding that students of color contort to be deemed successful • Throwing unprepared teachers into the classroom, especially in places where students need the most masterful, skilled, and qualified teachers • Racist, sexist, homophobic, transphobic, classist, paternalistic practices within schools, and the failure to eradicate such practices, beliefs, ideologies, and mindsets

RECOGNIZE AND REMOVE LOVELESS PRACTICES

A part of effectively loving our students requires that we peel back the layers and uncover the ways that, despite great intentions, schools are full of practices that are rooted in anti-Blackness, bias, and that are oppressive and truly . . . loveless.

In understanding domination and lovelessness in schools, at what point will we have the conversation around why there are so many white people driving learning outcomes and educational institutions for children who do not look like them? This is perhaps one of the largest forms of domination and expression of lack of love in schools.

PLEASE NOTE:
THOUGHTS ABOUT WHITE DOMINANT CULTURE

Throughout this text I speak about and against white dominant (or white supremacist) culture in schools. I'd like to offer deeper clarity on what this is and what it is not. When I train educators on white dominant culture in schools, I begin with the following questions:

What is white dominant or white supremacist culture? What comes to mind when you hear these terms? What do you hear? What images come to mind?

This line of questioning tends to reveal our varying ideas on what this means or could mean. Often it is rooted in images, sounds, and thoughts of white terror, racism, and violence, particularly of racist and inhumane acts during Jim Crow in the United States. Upon hearing this, many white educators feel deeply offended, attacked, or threatened. It is important to understand the multitude of ways that racism appears, is constructed, and is carried out within any society. Characteristics of white dominant culture include the norms, ideas, beliefs, practices, and actions deemed "right," "successful," or "appropriate" within a society. These aspects of culture are considered "white dominant or white supremacist" because they are rooted in Eurocentric or white ways being of being, dressing, speaking, and writing. Often, they are difficult to uproot because to achieve within American society—and in other communities globally—all of us must adapt, bend, or contort to these norms and ways of being if we want to "succeed."

Mainstream or popular ideas of success, beauty, intellect often dismiss or completely erase how cultures of the Global Majority—Black folx, Latinx folx, Asian folx, those of us who are not white—express, write, speak, heal, and what our ancestors defined as successful or as achievement. Specifically in schools, white dominant culture dictates practices such as:

- Grading policies:
  The very notion of grading a child's intellect feels inherently odd and uncreative, but in considering white dominant cultural norms, students often receive high grades or marks based on their ability to assimilate to or master what is deemed successful based on the white American culture of success. In some spaces, students who "behave" well receive higher grades. "Good" behavior is often defined as submission, silence, docility. Students also tend to receive higher grades when their work is "perfect." I must say that as a teacher I often struggled with how to navigate and move within existing structures and practices and often considered the reality of how to best engage with the profession in ways that would help and not harm my students. The education system is deliberate in making it difficult to resist.

- Academic language policies/prioritizing and praising the English language:
  Students whose first language is not English are essentially forced to assimilate. Although learning other languages is incredibly important for any child, students who have not "mastered" English are often demonized, penalized, or somehow viewed as not being as intelligent.

- How we respond to student culture and behavior:
  In some schools, students—especially Black students—are physically harmed. Some schools call the police on children. I worked in a school where staff, both white and

continues

nonwhite adults, encouraged and defended calling the police on a six-year-old student of color. There often exists in schools an approach to student culture and behavior that is deeply rooted in anti-Blackness. Students are penalized for their natural hair, the shapes of their bodies, the tones of their voices, and hand gestures or facial expressions that are simply part of who they are and how they express themselves. In some cases, students are punished for the trauma they hold due to their lived experiences. School culture often rewards silence and demonizes speech and cultures of children who are not white.

Figure 5.2 helps you to consider loveless practices in schools and what can be done by educators, both within and outside of the classroom, to create and sustain deeper spaces of love.

FIGURE 5.2 Loveless Practices in Schools and Ways to Cultivate Love

LOVELESS PRACTICES AND POLICIES IN SCHOOLS	WAYS TO CULTIVATE LOVE AS AN ADMINISTRATOR	WAYS TO CULTIVATE LOVE AS A TEACHER
White dominant culture in schools, which includes: • school culture and discipline policies that value silence and compliance • all, or predominantly, white staff especially in leadership, governance, or academic leadership roles • lack of creativity and critical thinking • cultures that nurture passive-aggressive responses and silence around racism and patriarchy rather than cultures of truthtelling.	• Honor and creating school cultures and climates that value truthtelling. • Center Black history and BIPOC histories throughout the school year rather than only doing so at certain times during the year. • Adopt, require that educators understand and can implement critical, anti-racist, antibias lenses. • Create cultures that are not paternalistic and racist. • Center student and community voices. • Diversify and truly listen to Black leaders who demonstrate a commitment to liberation (not all Black folx in leadership understand how to pursue liberation).	• Create and teach a curriculum that centers and honors students' histories, critical thinking, and the various ways that students learn and demonstrate information. • Center and activate student voices. Create student-led and student-centered classrooms. Create assignments and learning outputs that allow students to lead and share their thoughts and work. • Center student narratives. Allow students to write about themselves, be creative, tell their stories, and make connections to the content. • Celebrate and center the arts in instruction. • Study, research, and implement the work and practices of anti-racist, antibias, and culturally responsive scholars and practitioners. • Embody humility and learning from and alongside students.

FIGURE 5.2 Loveless Practices in Schools and Ways to Cultivate Love, *continued*

LOVELESS PRACTICES AND POLICIES IN SCHOOLS	WAYS TO CULTIVATE LOVE AS AN ADMINISTRATOR	WAYS TO CULTIVATE LOVE AS A TEACHER
Microaggressions, which include: • tone-policing staff and students (especially Black staff, Black women, and Black girls) • telling Black women and girls that the tones of their voices are aggressive or disrespectful • mispronouncing students' name or seeking to shorten students' names without permission • punishing students for ways of being that are connected to their culture (their speech, language, hair, attire, or body language) • heteronormative language, speech, and practices • a lack of gender-neutral language and scenarios • maintaining, excusing, or demanding low expectations for students, especially students of color.	• Center a commitment to ensuring that *all* educators, especially educators serving students of color, understand racial equity and what microaggressions are and how they show up in schools. • Center—over time, not just sometimes—professional development and training in anti-racism. • Create policies and systems that hold staff accountable for action and that corrects and repairs staff who regularly participate in racist behaviors, such as microaggressions. • Create and sustain spaces for staff of color who regularly experience microaggressions.	• Learn and correctly pronounce students' names; honor students' names and identities. • Develop a practice and lifestyle that help you understand forms of domination and harm, such as racism and sexism, including how they manifest within society, particularly in schools and how teachers can disrupt them. • Apologize and do better when you commit harm. • Teach students so that they are equipped with language and tools to disrupt. Center social justice. Teach critical theories and allow students to apply them to their lives and worlds. Create critical essential questions and enduring understandings so that students have the language and tools to critique and call out oppression. • Honor the totality of students' humanity. Teach the *whole* child. Consider students' human needs in the classroom. Tap into multiple learning styles. Get to know what excites students, what triggers students, what causes students' fears, and what gives them hope.

continues

FIGURE 5.2 Loveless Practices in Schools and Ways to Cultivate Love, *continued*

LOVELESS PRACTICES AND POLICIES IN SCHOOLS	WAYS TO CULTIVATE LOVE AS AN ADMINISTRATOR	WAYS TO CULTIVATE LOVE AS A TEACHER
Predominantly white teachers and leaders	• Center efforts to recruit, diversify, *and retain* educators of color. • Create pipelines and pathways for educators to move into all forms of educational leadership. • Encourage some white educators and leaders who are not committed to liberation to leave or move into other roles. • Create environments that center the totality of educators of color, including removing barriers to positions for educators in schools. • Pay educators well. • Invest in the wellness of educators, especially those of color.	If you are a white teacher serving students of color: • Check the ways that you may be operating from, within, or benefiting from white privilege and seek to correct this behavior. • If you are not centering the liberation of BIPOC students and communities, perhaps you may want to reconsider/consider your purposes for teaching. • Ensure that you are a lifelong learner of BIPOC students' histories and the students' present, and that you are working to be a coconspirator in the work of liberation. • Be humble and teachable. Own your mistakes. Encourage mistakes. Lead by example in this way. • Apologize when you do harm. • Commit to a lifestyle of understanding and working toward liberation. • Do not assume that you are an expert on Black culture or Black students, *ever*. Always seek to learn with and from your students.

FIGURE 5.2 Loveless Practices in Schools and Ways to Cultivate Love, *continued*

LOVELESS PRACTICES AND POLICIES IN SCHOOLS	WAYS TO CULTIVATE LOVE AS AN ADMINISTRATOR	WAYS TO CULTIVATE LOVE AS A TEACHER
Curriculum that does not take into account the various and rich ways that all students, particularly BIPOC students, learn Curriculum violence—a practice coined by Stephanie Jones—including the ways that teachers, specifically, inflict harm on students through lessons, simulations, and content that are traumatizing, triggering, outright wrong or harmful	• Move away from purchasing curriculum—often from white vendors—that does not center culturally responsive, antibias, or anti-racist teaching and learning. • Invest in training and professional development that equips teachers with the tools, practices, and skill sets to teach and design curriculum that centers liberation. • Invest in high-quality, highly experienced teachers who are experts in their content and pedagogical practices. • Support teacher well-being so that highly qualified teachers will remain in schools. • Know and understand what committing curriculum violence is so that harm is not inflicted through curriculum. • Create practices and policies that hold teachers and leaders accountable for curriculum violence and teach educators how to do better and how to repair harm in the classroom if it happens.	• Do *your* work. Research curriculum violence to ensure you are not committing it. • Ask questions and study when you are uncertain. • Always ask yourself and other educators whether something will be harmful before you implement. • Seek resources, such as *Learning for Justice* and the work of scholar educators such as Stephanie Jones, Gholdy Muhammad, Lisa Delpit, Gloria Ladson-Billings, and Bettina Love. • Consider multiple ways that you might approach teaching hard history and other content that may be challenging for students to digest. • Invest in *truly* knowing who your students are so that you can plan and implement your instruction accordingly and in culturally responsive and trauma-informed ways. • Apologize when you do harm and do better!

continues

FIGURE 5.2 Loveless Practices in Schools and Ways to Cultivate Love, *continued*

LOVELESS PRACTICES AND POLICIES IN SCHOOLS	WAYS TO CULTIVATE LOVE AS AN ADMINISTRATOR	WAYS TO CULTIVATE LOVE AS A TEACHER
Leaders who prioritize their political or professional gain or advancement over the needs of students, which looks like: • leaders moving into roles simply to advance their careers or to gain politically and at the expense of children • leaders making decisions not in the best interest of children, but because they are seeking to gain in other ways.	• Create pipelines and pathways that properly vet educational leaders, particularly in ways that are rooted in liberation. • Eliminate gatekeeping systems, policies, and practices that allow the same types of leaders to assume leadership roles and schools. • Create committees and processes that are equitable, rooted in liberation, and honor all stakeholders (caregivers/parents, students, and teachers) in selecting leaders, not just leaders with the same agendas selecting other leaders who will uphold the same problematic agendas. • *Consider another profession if your purpose in education is to advance politically by exploiting children.* • Create pathways to selecting leaders that honor intersectional justice. • Normalize integrity, humility, and truthtelling in selecting and retaining leaders. • Create support systems so that educators of color do not feel that they must contort to lead well in schools.	• Advocate for leaders that are liberation minded. • Create committees and teams that allow educators to advocate as a collective so that no one feels that they have to advocate alone. • Hold leaders accountable to and for integrity and truthtelling. • Have courageous conversations with leaders in ways that will hold them accountable. • Mobilize students so that they feel equipped and protected in pushing back against leaders who are seeking to exploit them for their own interests or gain.

FIGURE 5.2 Loveless Practices in Schools and Ways to Cultivate Love, *continued*

LOVELESS PRACTICES AND POLICIES IN SCHOOLS	WAYS TO CULTIVATE LOVE AS AN ADMINISTRATOR	WAYS TO CULTIVATE LOVE AS A TEACHER
Schools and school leaders driven largely by capitalism are deeply anti-love. When schools and leaders place value on monetary gain and advancement over the needs of children, this leads to all types of issues, such as: • ineffective and underqualified leaders remaining in place • white folx being sustained in power, especially in schools serving mostly students of color • measures of success remaining tied to outcomes such as standardized data that uphold and reinforce other racist, harmful practices in schools.	• Normalize building and creating schools that truly are created for the purposes of loving children. • Examine the ways that capitalism is harmful in and on schools and actively work against this. • Move away from prioritizing standardized exams and other data rooted in whiteness that promote and uphold capitalism and are harmful to students as a result. • Center liberatory practices in professional development and training so that all staff have a consciousness on how to work against all forms of domination. • Implement staff readings and learning groups that focus specifically on how schools driven by capitalism are harmful.	• Advocate for leaders that are liberation minded. • Create committees and teams that allow educators to advocate as a collective so that no one feels that they have to advocate alone. • Hold leaders accountable to and for integrity and truthtelling. • Have courageous conversations with leaders in ways that will hold them accountable. • Mobilize students so that they feel equipped and protected in pushing back against leaders who are seeking to exploit them for their own interests or gain. • Expand your knowledge of liberatory practices so that you are able to advocate for liberatory practices in schools.

continues

FIGURE 5.2 Loveless Practices in Schools and Ways to Cultivate Love, *continued*

LOVELESS PRACTICES AND POLICIES IN SCHOOLS	WAYS TO CULTIVATE LOVE AS AN ADMINISTRATOR	WAYS TO CULTIVATE LOVE AS A TEACHER
Patriarchy, sexism, and paternalism To achieve liberation, schools must also consider how patriarchy and sexism are forms of domination and are ultimately loveless. In schools, this looks like: • overwhelming numbers of men, or an overwhelming patriarchal presence in school decision-making • an overreliance on or a belief in the influence men, specifically cisgender, heterosexual men, to hold and exert power • failure to penalize or eradicate toxic masculinity • men leaders stealing the ideas of women, or using women's ideas and refusing to give them credit • normalizing homophobic or sexualized language and play that are harmful to women and girls, gender nonconforming, and queer individuals • "boys only" meetings, spaces, and conduct • failing to hold men accountable for bad behavior • failing to include conversations on patriarchy and sexism in equity trainings and professional development.	• Create schools that are safe for women, girls, and gender-expansive youth. • Hold men accountable. • Ensure that efforts to achieve equity in schools also include teaching, learning about, and disrupting patriarchy and sexist practices. • Ensure that there are policies and measures of accountability for individuals upholding or participating in harmful behaviors. • Normalize holding staff accountable for working against all forms of oppression. • Create cultures where women and girls feel safe advocating for themselves. • Ensure that men are held responsible for stealing the ideas of other people, including women (in the same way teachers hold students accountable for plagiarizing). • Ensure that men of color understand the importance of their role in sexist behaviors. Often, this is a difficult conversation, especially for Black men, as they experience oppression due to racism. Hold them accountable anyway.	• Create learning environments that are safe for women and girls. • Teach students. Equip students with the language and tools to hold one another accountable, to advocate for themselves, and to resist. • Teach students about intersectionality, patriarchy, and sexism to equip them with tools to know and do better. • Do not brush toxic masculinity under the rug as "normal" behavior for boys. • Model caring for women and girls through word and deed.

FIGURE 5.2 Loveless Practices in Schools and Ways to Cultivate Love, *continued*

LOVELESS PRACTICES AND POLICIES IN SCHOOLS	WAYS TO CULTIVATE LOVE AS AN ADMINISTRATOR	WAYS TO CULTIVATE LOVE AS A TEACHER

Internalized racism and oppression
 	
This is always a tough piece to teach because people of color, especially Black people, experience oppression. However, to move toward love, we have to understand all of the ways that racism manifests, and this includes the internalized beliefs, practices, and mindsets that folx of color can and do develop as a result of living within a culture that praises and rewards whiteness. I will also note that this is difficult because some people of color feel that they must continue some of the behaviors listed to be "successful" or to advance in schools.
 	
In schools this looks like:
 	
- folx of color participating in behaviors, practices, and speech that are rooted in racism, such as
  – colorism
  – tone-policing
  – policing hair styles, gestures, and facial expressions
  – demonizing other folx of color who choose to resist
  – perpetuating racist and white dominant cultural practices either from a place of ignorance or of being the "good" person of color to achieve or get ahead
  – enabling white or people of color leaders who are harming other people.
	- Include internalized racism and oppression in the equity work that we say we do in schools.
	- Teach and educate about this so folx are aware and are able to correct, repair, adjust, and heal.
	- Do not throw Black folx, especially, into places of leadership without understanding their beliefs and mindsets with regard to liberation. Many leaders of color do great harm because they uphold the "master's" agenda and use the "master's tools."[4]
	- Ensure that anti-racist measures, efforts, and practices include internalized racism.
	- Create and hold space for folx of color to name and work through the ways we can harm one another.
	- Create space for coalition and community building, especially with regard to anti-Blackness in many cultures and communities.
	- Create a learning environment among staff and students that cultivates self-love.
		- Educate yourself on the ways that people of color internalize oppression and racism and how this can manifest among young people. Sometimes educators dismiss this as bullying without understanding or working to heal the root causes.
		- Teach! Teach students about internalized oppression and racism in ways that they can access. Encourage students to know that they can do something about it.
		- Create a learning environment rooted in exploring identity, self-love, and belonging.

continues

FIGURE 5.2 Loveless Practices in Schools and Ways to Cultivate Love, *continued*

LOVELESS PRACTICES AND POLICIES IN SCHOOLS	WAYS TO CULTIVATE LOVE AS AN ADMINISTRATOR	WAYS TO CULTIVATE LOVE AS A TEACHER
Homophobia and transphobia	• Engage in your own and continuous learning about LGBTQIA+ communities. • Center professional development, training, and cultures around LGBTQIA+ communities. • Create policies and practices that ensure all students are cared for, seen, and safe. • Do not ostracize queer, nonbinary, or gender-expansive youth or staff. • Encourage celebrations, community events, and advocacy measures designed to celebrate identity, love, and diverse experiences.	• Be mindful to use gender-expansive language. • Acknowledge and seek to do better when using language and examples that are heteronormative. • Allow students to share their pronouns and how they choose to identity. • Create a classroom community rooted in care and belonging. • Center articles and texts that reflect varying experiences and identities. • Lead by example. • Correct and repair harmful language and behavior.
Toxic grind cultures and burnout	• Create cultures that honor rest and self-care. • Be a leader who practices self-care, thereby reinforcing a staff and student culture where people feel that it is normal to care for themselves, to rest, to set boundaries, and to use "No" as a complete sentence. • Consider how to have staff work smarter and not always harder. • Encourage collaboration and a community of care. • Advocate for adequate and respectable teacher pay. • Advocate for enough time off for staff. • Lead by example.	• Confront mindsets you hold that suggest that self-care is selfish. • Allow students to have breaks. • Be mindful of the amount of outside work that is being assigned for students and determine the source of the need for this work. • Be clear about whether students need to produce more work. Consider if there are systemic issues rooted in oppression that you are seeking to address by making students work harder. • Create learning assignments and demonstrations of learning that are engaging and culturally responsive and stretch student thinking.

This list is not exhaustive. Not every harmful practice that exists in schools is named here, but it can begin to explain the ways schools reinforce systems, ideas, beliefs, and actions that are rooted in domination and are anti-love.

DEVELOP COMMUNITIES BUILT UPON LOVING BLACK CHILDREN

When I think of communities built upon loving Black children, I think about my first school and my first teacher: my mother. My mother—who did not have the opportunity for formal higher education and often said that she was not a good student—deeply believes in education and instilled a love for reading and school in me and my siblings very early on. My first lesson on Black history, on knowing and loving who I was and from where I came, despite our impoverished surroundings, all came from my mother. She understood what Black children needed and sought to instill in us all we would need to do more than well in this world. The first elementary school that I attended was an arts impact school, a public school in Columbus, Ohio, where I did not have a white teacher until fifth grade. When I did encounter white teachers, I knew that they saw me and they loved me. Even still, before that point I had a foundation in education that was rooted in my being seen, in Black excellence, in Black history, and in a community that loved me.

PLEASE NOTE: MY PERSPECTIVE

I acknowledge that my perspective is not entirely inclusive to all marginalized groups and experiences. I do believe in and know that when we focus on the most marginalized within any society, which I would argue in the United States includes Black communities, our desires to heal, to eradicate oppression, ultimately creates liberatory solutions and practices for all who are marginalized. I hope that educators will be able to use examples centered on Black children to build and curate spaces of love for all children, particularly those who are often relegated to the margins of society.

I had the privilege of attending Spelman College, an institution built around, for, and dedicated toward loving Black women, a curated space where Black women can love themselves without abandon. My experience there, and being able to pay witness to the result of attending an institution that loves Black women and

Black people, has provided me with an understanding of how to build and sustain learning communities within education that are built upon loving Black children.

Create Space and Time to Imagine, to Curate, to Build

If educators are seeking to contribute to the world in positive ways that require young people to view their worlds critically and do something about it, we have to first curate spaces where students feel loved, seen, and nourished. There is an expectation that young people produce and give when our educational systems are loveless places where many students, particularly Black students, are malnourished.

Educators, therefore, have to be given room, space, and encouragement to consider what is not working in our schools; time to read, research, and study; and time to work with colleagues and experts who *know* what it looks like and means to create spaces that love Black children.

Schools can work to achieve this in many ways:

- Utilize teacher professional development and planning time more intentionally and in ways that are rooted in liberation.
- Provide space and time for educators, especially teachers, to ask questions and push back—often schools are paternalistic and seek to keep teachers silent, which is deeply problematic, as *good* teachers are the most equipped to share ideas and practices that will both lead to deeper learning/successful academic outcomes and liberatory practices.
- Diversify professional development options. Allow different staff members to lead and determine training needs.
- Be more thoughtful and allow others to drive ideas around how teachers will spend prep time over the summer before returning to teaching.
- Assign more critical texts for all-staff readings that will actually lead toward liberation.
- Eliminate toxic grind culture.
- Find solutions and ways around or approaches that can lessen the demand for standardized testing:
  - Find consortiums within states that allow schools to opt out of standardized testing (e.g., in New York City, schools can become project-based learning schools, exempt from standardized tests).
  - Mobilize parents. Parents have great political power in education. Parents can also choose to opt students out of standardized testing.

- · For teachers who wish to, forming teacher-advocacy groups or committees with the specific goal of working toward liberation is a small, yet might way for teachers to lead this work. Teachers should also receive stipends for additional work.
- ▪ Teachers can create this kind of space in the classroom by:
  - · Assigning more meaningful assignments, not simply packets or busy work. As I became a stronger, more intentional, and critical teacher, I was intentional about decreasing the amount of work I asked students to complete outside of the classroom and worked to build more rigorous, project-based, critical student-centered learning in class.

HEALING, BELONGING, AND SPREADING LOVE

Whenever movements of resistance center those who are harmed most in a society (in many societies this includes descendants of enslaved African people, Black, poor, queer, trans women and girls, those of us whose aspects of our identity and lived experiences cause us to experience overlapping and simultaneous forms of oppression), humanity moves closer to collective liberation. This emphasis is not meant to create a debate around a hierarchy of oppression or who has it hardest within society, but to honor and acknowledge intersectional injustice and its impact on Black children specifically. Our efforts and aims to resist, transform, and liberate are beneficial to each of us.

Intersectional justice, therefore, is needed in our efforts to ensure liberation because when we focus on those who are most oppressed within any society, we are better positioned to move to a place where everyone is free, where love abounds.

The authors of *The Combahee River Collective Statement* further articulate the role of Black women's freedom, of intersectional justice, as an integral part of liberation: "If Black women were free, it would mean that everyone else would have to be free since our freedom would necessitate the destruction of all the systems of oppression."[5]

I want the practice of teaching, the field of education, to be about love. I choose to believe that educators are drawn to the field and remain in it because there is a love for children. James Baldwin is one of the most prolific voices on race relations in America. I am often drawn to his work and words because of the honesty with which he describes what racism sounds like, looks like, and feels like and because he *always* goes back to the root of love. The scholarship of bell hooks is similar in this way, and she offers similar guidance—we need love to achieve collective liberation.

When we truly love ourselves, we do not seek to dominate others. When we are clear on who we are, and we believe in the power of our unique being and purpose, we do not seek to be in education for our own benefit or to use our careers for political or monetary gain. When we love ourselves, we do not seek to put women down or to assert our power over them or children, who are the most vulnerable within our society. When we love ourselves, truly, we do not seek to prove our worthiness by engaging in practices that silence people, that are manipulative or controlling. When we love ourselves, we are able to operate from a high vibration rooted in healing, belonging, and spreading love.

In this way, *love* is the most powerful force in moving us *toward liberation*.

QUESTIONS FOR TEACHERS TO CONSIDER

1. What do you need to work against domination and toward love?
2. How can you love yourself more deeply?
3. How can you love your students more deeply?
4. How can you shift towards centering liberation in your educational practice?

ACKNOWLEDGMENTS

There is much to acknowledge and many to thank. I must acknowledge the Source, my Source, from which I receive the most profound guidance, truth, grace, gentleness, power, and courage to be a vessel and a voice. My mother, whose love, strength, courage, and example has birthed in me all that I have needed to get to this point. I must also acknowledge the educational spaces and community spaces that held and saw me most as a child. The teachers who allowed me to teach, those who spoke and acted in ways that were life-giving. Those who created spaces for me to flourish and sojourn. I am grateful, too, for the instruction that this life—thus far—has offered, the moments and hardships that I remember and carry in my core that both birth and sustain a fire for justice, the eradication of oppression, and righteousness. I know, truly, from where and whence I came and acknowledge the ways that my path, which has been an exceptional one despite the poverty and forms of oppression that have been levied against me and those who look like me, has been an intentional one.

I acknowledge the role and place of Spelman College and the nurturing, powerful, educational space that has poured so much into me. For the nonconforming, truthtelling, beautiful Black women and sisters who continue to show and pave the way.

I can extend thanks to the ancestors, the shoulders on which I stand. I know that I am because we are.

I extend deep gratitude to my students, whom I have had the privilege to teach, lead, guide, and learn from throughout the past decade. Thank you for your trust. Your patience. Your guidance. Your leadership. For creating space.

To my friends and family—dearest ones—for your encouragement, love, support, wisdom, and all of the ways that you see me. Thank you.

May this work be one that holds and uplifts each of us.

NOTES

INTRODUCTION
1. Baldwin, "A Talk to Teachers."
2. Walker, *In Search of Our Mothers' Gardens*.

CHAPTER ONE: TEACHING AS TRUTHTELLING
1. Baldwin, "The Precarious Vogue of Ingmar Bergman."
2. Baldwin, "A Talk to Teachers" speech.
3. hooks, "Love as the Practice of Freedom," 243–45.
4. Lorde, "The Master's Tools Will Never Dismantle the Master's House," 102.
5. Love, *We Want to Do More Than Survive*, 11.
6. Kim, "What Critical Race Theory Is, and What It Means for Teachers."

CHAPTER TWO: TEACHING AS ACTIVISM
1. Baldwin, "A Talk to Teachers."
2. Douglass, "Blessings of Liberty and Education."
3. Muhammad, *Cultivating Genius*.

CHAPTER THREE: TEACHING AS HEALING
1. Coates, *Between the World and Me*, 10.
2. Baldwin, *The Fire Next Time*, 18.
3. Jones, "Ending Curriculum Violence."

CHAPTER FOUR: HEALING AND SELF-CARE FOR TEACHERS
1. Pitts, "Students Lose When Black Women Aren't Supported."
2. Hurston, *Their Eyes Were Watching God*, 138.
3. Pitts, "Students Lose When Black Women Aren't Supported."
4. Lorde, *A Burst of Light*, 131.

CHAPTER FIVE: TEACHING AS LOVE
1. Pitts, "What Anti-Racism Really Means for Educators." Emphasis in original.
2. hooks, "Love as the Practice of Freedom," 243–44.
3. hooks, "Love as the Practice of Freedom," 293.

4. As Audre Lorde observed, "For the master's tools will never dismantle the master's house. They may allow us to temporarily beat him at his own game, but they will never enable us to bring about genuine change." I once worked for some school leaders of color who believed this anti-liberation idea that they could use the master's tools to get ahead as people of color within oppressive systems. Many people of color believe in and use this idea to succeed in some respects, but it ultimately moves us away from collective liberation. Lorde, "The Master's Tools Will Never Dismantle the Master's House."

5. *The Combahee River Collective Statement.*

WORKS CITED

Alarcón, Francisco X. and Odilia Galván Rodríguez, eds. *Poetry of Resistance: Voices for Social Justice.* Foreword by Juan Felipe Herrera. Tucson: University of Arizona Press, 2016.

Baldwin, James. *The Fire Next Time.* New York: Dial Press, 1963.

———. "A Letter to My Nephew." *The Progressive,* December 1, 1962.

———. "The Precarious Vogue of Ingmar Bergman." *Esquire,* April 1, 1960; republished as "The Northern Protestant" in *Nobody Knows My Name: More Notes of a Native Son* (New York: Dial Press, 1961) and in *The Price of the Ticket: Collected Nonfiction 1948–1985* (New York: St. Martin's Press, 1985).

———. "A Talk to Teachers." Speech delivered October 16, 1963, as "The Negro Child—His Self-Image," published in *The Saturday Review,* December 21, 1963, and reprinted in *The Price of the Ticket: Collected Nonfiction, 1948–1985.*

brown, adrienne maree. *Emergent Strategy: Shaping Change, Changing Worlds.* Chico, CA: AK Press, 2017.

———. *Pleasure Activism: The Politics of Feeling Good.* Chico, CA: AK Press, 2019.

Coates, Ta-Nehisi. *Between the World and Me.* New York: Spiegel & Grau, 2015.

The Combahee River Collective Statement. Women's and Gender Studies Web Archive (165), April 1977. Washington, DC: Library of Congress, 2015. https://www.loc.gov/item/lcwaN0028151.

Crenshaw, Kimberlé. "Demarginalizing the Intersection of Race and Sex: A Black Feminist Critique of Antidiscrimination Doctrine, Feminist Theory and Antiracist Politics." *University of Chicago Legal Forum* 1989, issue 1, article 8 (1989). https://chicagounbound.uchicago.edu/cgi/viewcontent.cgi?article=1052&context=uclf.

Delpit, Lisa. *"Multiplication Is for White People": Raising Expectations for Other People's Children.* New York: New Press, 2012.

Douglass, Frederick. "Blessings of Liberty and Education." Speech, delivered September 3, 1894, https://teachingamericanhistory.org/document/blessings -of-liberty-and-education/. Accessed February 10, 2022.

Freire, Paulo. *Pedagogy of the Oppressed.* 30th anniversary ed. Translated by Myra Bergman Ramos. New York: Continuum, 2000.

hooks, bell. "Love as the Practice of Freedom." In *Outlaw Culture: Resisting Representations.* Independence, KY: Routledge & Kegan Paul, 1994.

———. *Outlaw Culture: Resisting Representations.* Independence, KY: Routledge & Kegan Paul, 1994.

———. *Teaching to Transgress: Education as the Practice of Freedom.* New York: Routledge, 1994.

Horton, Myles, and Paulo Freire. *We Make the Road by Walking: Conversations on Education and Social Change.* Philadelphia: Temple University Press, 1990.

Hurston, Zora Neale. *Their Eyes Were Watching God.* Philadelphia: J. B. Lippincott, 1937.

Jones, Stephanie P. "Ending Curriculum Violence." *Learning for Justice.* Southern Poverty Law Center, Spring 2020. https://www.learningforjustice.org /magazine/spring-2020/ending-curriculum-violence.

Kim, Bob. "What Critical Race Theory Is, and What It Means for Teachers." *Heinemann Blog*, August 9, 2021. https://blog.heinemann.com/critical-race -theory-q-and-a.

Ladson-Billings, Gloria. *The Dreamkeepers: Successful Teachers of African American Children.* San Francisco: Jossey-Bass, 1994.

Lorde, Audre. *A Burst of Light: And Other Essays.* Ithaca, NY: Firebrand Books, 1988.

———. *The Master's Tools Will Never Dismantle the Master's House.* London: Penguin Classics, 2018.

Love, Bettina L. *We Want to Do More Than Survive: Abolitionist Teaching and the Pursuit of Educational Freedom.* Boston: Beacon Press, 2019.

Morris, Monique W. *Pushout: The Criminalization of Black Girls in Schools.* New York: New Press, 2016.

———. *Sing a Rhythm, Dance a Blues: Education for the Liberation of Black and Brown Girls.* New York: New Press, 2019.

Morrison, Toni. *Beloved.* Originally published 1987. Pimlico: Vintage Classics, 2007.

Muhammad, Gholdy. *Cultivating Genius: An Equity Framework for Culturally and Historically Responsive Literacy.* New York: Scholastic, 2020.

National Governors Association Center for Best Practices, Council of Chief State School Officers. *Common Core State Standards.* Washington, DC: National Governors Association Center for Best Practices, Council of Chief State School Officers, 2010.

Pitts, Jamilah. "Students Lose When Black Women Aren't Supported." *Learning for Justice.* Southern Poverty Law Center, November 15, 2021. https://www.learningforjustice.org/magazine/students-lose-when-black-women-arent-supported.

———. "What Anti-Racism Really Means for Educators." *Learning for Justice.* Southern Poverty Law Center, September 11, 2020. https://www.learningforjustice.org/magazine/what-antiracism-really-means-for-educators.

Steinmetz, Katy. "She Coined the Term 'Intersectionality' Over 30 Years Ago. Here's What It Means to Her Today." *Time,* February 20, 2020. https://time.com/5786710/kimberle-crenshaw-intersectionality.

Taylor, Keeanga-Yamahtta, ed. *How We Get Free: Black Feminism and the Combahee River Collective.* Chicago: Haymarket Books, 2017.

"Universal Declaration of Human Rights." United Nations, 1948. https://www.un.org/en/about-us/universal-declaration-of-human-rights.

Waheed, Nayyirah. *salt.* San Bernardino, CA: CreateSpace Independent Publishing Platform, 2019.

Walker, Alice. *In Search of Our Mothers' Gardens.* San Diego: Harcourt Brace Jovanovich, 1983.

Woodson, Carter Godwin. *The Mis-Education of the Negro.* Trenton, NJ: Africa World Press, 1990.

ABOUT THE AUTHOR

Jamilah Pitts is an educator, a social entrepreneur, a writer, and a wellness educator whose work centers the liberation, healing, and holistic development of communities of the Global Majority. Jamilah has worked and served in various roles and spaces to promote racial justice and healing, including as a teacher, a coach, a dean, and an assistant principal. She has worked in domestic and international educational spaces in Massachusetts, New York, the Dominican Republic, China, and India.

As the founder and CEO of Jamilah Pitts Consulting, Jamilah partners with schools, communities, universities, and organizations to advance the work of racial, social, and intersectional justice through training, coaching, strategic planning, and curriculum design. Jamilah is also the founder of She, Imprints, an organization serving at the intersection of wellness and justice for women and girls of the Global Majority.

Jamilah's written work has appeared in *Huffington Post*, *Learning for Justice*, and *EdWeek*. She has spoken to audiences of thousands of educators both within the United States and internationally. Jamilah threads her passion for human rights and social justice into her teaching, writing, scholarship, and artistic pursuits. Jamilah sees education and healing as her life's work and calling, and she truly believes that education should be an avenue through which empathy, healing, and justice are promoted.

Jamilah is certified as a yoga teacher and Reiki practitioner, and she is certified in the Trauma-Conscious Yoga Method.

Jamilah is a proud alumna of Spelman College, where she earned a bachelor of arts in English. Jamilah also pursued graduate studies at Boston College and Teachers College, Columbia University.

Jamilah has served on the *Learning for Justice* advisory board and is a Fund for Teachers Fellow, a UNCF Education Fellow, and an Institute for Citizens and Scholars Fellow.

Jamilah is an avid traveler, a dancer, and a serious foodie.